The Lemon Tree

Artists' & Writers' Personal Journeys of Creativity

Edited by Nitza Agam

Copyright © 2022 by Nitza Agam

All rights reserved. No part of this publication may be reproduced, distributed or transmitted in any form or by any means, including photocopying, recording, or other electronic or mechanical methods, without the prior written permission of the publisher, except in the case of brief quotations embodied in critical reviews and certain other noncommercial uses permitted by copyright law. For permission requests, write to the publisher, addressed "Attention: Permissions Coordinator," at the address below.

Boss Lady Press
40 FM 1960 West, #141
Houston, TX 77090
info@bossladypress.com

Book Design & Layout: Darshell McAlpine, Boss Lady Press
Cover Art: Avigile Gottlieb
Author Photograph: Abby Caplin

The Lemon Tree: Artists' & Writers' Personal Journeys of Creativity
ISBN: 978-1-7355922-2-0
Library of Congress Control Number:2022900302

In memory of my beloved friend and kindred spirit

Annette Walt

"The Lemon Tree" was inspired by the women's newsletter, "Women's Work," which was a way to collect many of these essays and works of art. Many thanks to all the women who contributed and to Rebecca Mikosz for her expertise and dedication.

A special thank you to Jennifer Vaida for her editing and her knack for perfection.

This anthology could not come to life without the inspired and visionary Darshell McAlpine who published it with Boss Lady Press.

Finally, a thank you to the artistry of Avigile Gottlieb who captured the delicate fragility and strength of The Lemon Tree on the cover.

To the spirit of women artists and writers, my mother, Naomi, and my husband, Ofer Agam, and sons, David and Orr Agam.

Contents

Untitled - Annette Walt ... i

Introduction - Nitza Agam ... ii

Untitled - Annette Walt ... iii

Crocus - Dawn Winder ... iv

For Annette: Artist and Friend - Nitza Agam ... 1

In Bloom - Barbara Greensweig ... 2

Giants, Fairies & Foxes—Oh My! - Leigh Verrill-Rhys ... 3

Moon Phase - Alison Trujillo ... 7

Annette's Garden - Marisa Handler ... 8

San Miguel - Barbara Greensweig ... 10

Summer of 1972 - Susan E. Light ... 11

Boil - Jennifer Ewing ... 15

Half Moon - Alison Trujillo ... 16

Poetry Medicine - Abby Caplin ... 17

Limpet Nation 2 - Alison Trujillo ... 19

Untitled - Annette Walt ... 20

Women's Work - Nitza Agam ... 21

Half Moon Bay Nursery Interior - Barbara Greensweig ... 24

Friend Me - Marlene Shigekawa ... 25

Sparkle - Jennifer Ewing ... 29

My Death According to Poetry - Doreen Stock ... 30

Bella Luna - Gretchen Butler ... 32

A Love Story - Darshell McAlpine ... 33

Autumn Afternoon - Barbara Greensweig ... 36

The Balancing Act - Barbara Greensweig ... 37

Golden Bird - Gretchen Butler … *40*

Stories and Moving Pictures - Marlene Shigekawa … *41*

Holy Water, The Ganges, Varanasi, India - Barbara Greensweig … *44*

Thoughts on Being an Asian American Woman Writer . . . - Cynthia Chin-Lee … *45*

The Space Between Us - Barbara Greensweig … *49*

Lemon tree - Avigile Gottlieb … *50*

The Lemon Tree - Nitza Agam … *51*

Limpet Nation 1 - Alison Trujillo … *53*

Ice Canyon - Jennifer Ewing … *54*

How Art Has Made All the Difference - Jennifer Ewing … *55*

Sword Fern - Alison Trujillo … *59*

Beacon of Light - Barbara Greensweig … *60*

Pictures in the Sky - Kathleen Meadows … *61*

Backyard Garden - Barbara Greensweig … *64*

Essential Goods - Jennifer Fowler Vaida … *65*

Changing Woman Navajo Myth - Gretchen Butler … *68*

Art Round-Up - Gretchen Butler … *69*

Path - Jennifer Ewing … *72*

My Own Diary - Nitza Agam … *73*

Woman Rising, Women Honoring Sii (Water) - Catherine Herrera … *76*

How the Spirit of Creativity Moves Me - Catherine Herrera … *77*

Grotte - Jennifer Ewing … *81*

To the Moon - Abby Caplin … *82*

Moon Over Taos - Alison Trujillo … *84*

Following D.H. Lawrence - Nitza Agam … *85*

Aqua Corraline - Alison Trujillo … *88*

To the Creatives - Alison Trujillo … *89*

Pumpkin Pickup - Barbara Greensweig 91

Green River - Jennifer Ewing 92

A Beautiful Life - Angela Neff 93

Summer Sunflowers, Taos - Alison Trujillo 95

Below the Mountains - Alison Trujillo 96

The Changing Light - Kathleen Meadows 97

Biographies 98

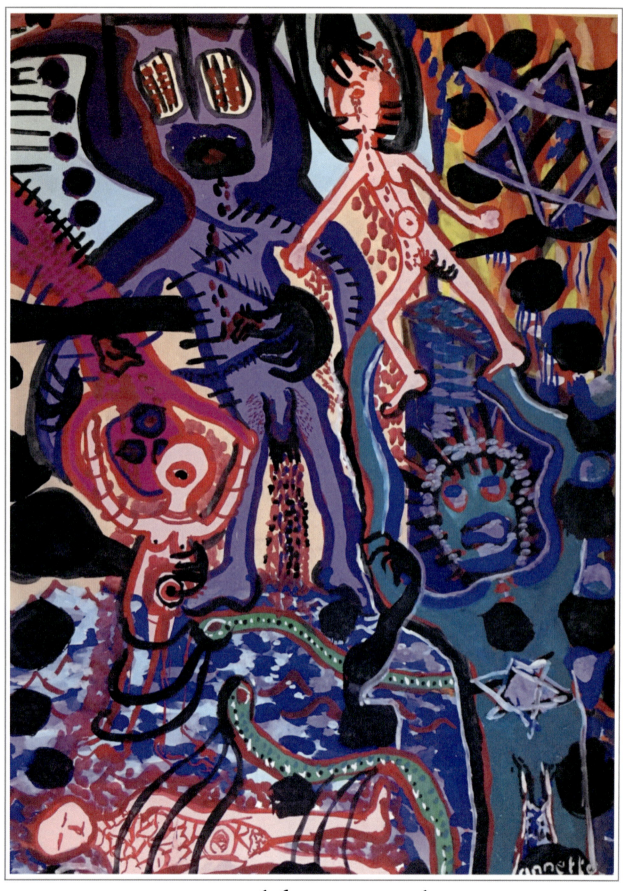

Untitled, Annette Walt

Introduction

I began writing when I was eight years old and received a birthday gift of a Girl Scout Journal which was titled, "My Own Diary," with the picture of a girl scout in her uniform, blonde-haired and white, resembling a kind of Barbie doll, chewing on a pen, and an open diary on her desk. The symbol of the Girl Scouts was above the title. That was it for me. The beginning of my life as a writer, and as a young girl, to a teenager, to a young woman, to a mother, to middle age, and to now, as a 70-year-old. Throughout my life, I felt it important to document my life, to archive the events and the joys and tragedies, and it was fine if I was the only audience for those words, those moments. In time, journals became my tool for understanding myself, for articulating what was important, and in a way, to preserve those moments that seem to end quickly. They laid the foundation for me as a writer, a poet, a teacher, a mother, a dreamer, a seeker.

It was not enough, however, to write alone and to be alone. The words were a comfort, but I craved community. I wanted other people, and mostly women, who shared my experiences, to speak to, to share, to mirror. While living in Israel, I became part of an autobiographical women's theatre company, and we acted out our lives. The play, "Women about Women," performed in the attic of a theatre or on various stages in small towns or small theaters became a hit. I witnessed the power of lived experience through the word and through the performance.

The impetus for this anthology emerged when my best friend passed away, and I discovered hidden art in her attic comprising hundreds of paintings in thick, taped portfolios. Visions of her inner world in bright, bold colors and archetypal images seemed to reach off the paper, which was over thirty years old. I had discovered another hidden part of my friend and one she felt she could not share. I was happy to find them, to become the curator of her art, but sad that she did not share any of them during our friendship. I thought of so many women poets, writers, artists, through the ages who, like her, hid their art, or put them away somewhere, only to be found after their death. As a writer, a friend, an actress, a teacher, a museum tour guide, I began reaching out to my women friends to see what their stories were. How did they feel about their art and writing? When did they know they had something to share or to hide? What were those stories of their creativity and their need to express themselves? The essays, poems, artwork, and stories could not come fast enough once I made my request.

Marlene Shikegawa remembered as a Japanese American girl growing up near L.A., seeing her drawings made from colored crayons hanging in the cafeteria with other drawings. Suddenly, she was being "seen" for the first time, this black-haired girl where mostly blonde-haired, blue-eyed classmates' drawings hung on the wall. Jennifer Ewing held fast to her artistic passions despite her father's desire to see her become a mathematician. Gretchen Butler began sketching egg beaters in her kitchen while her toddler took a nap. Her art became increasingly more complex, whimsical, and untraditional.

Cynthia Chin-Lee, inspired by her mother's talent as a visual artist and storyteller, but not able to pursue her dreams, moves Cynthia to share the stories of her community and others who might not fit in. Kathleen Meadows spent long days lying in alfalfa fields in the Central Valley of California, gazing up at the sky, using her imagination to transcend her farm and plan a life of adventures and art.

Each woman's story or poem in the anthology, "The Lemon Tree" shares the hope, the triumph, the frustrations, the overcoming of obstacles, and the comfort and inspiration that their art provided for them. We are women of all ages and backgrounds and share our memories of how we knew we had a story to tell. It is the "hard copy" not the digital one or the one on a screen but one that fills the pages of this book that can be held, examined, read, discussed, and shown.

I hope you, the reader, finds one or more of these moments in time that resonates with you, and may prompt you to think about yourself. And while you may choose not to share your art or writing, it will not lie in an attic, unseen, or in a drawer, ignored. Even a small part of that story remains important and becomes part of our collective women's heritage.

Crocus

Dawn Gibson-Winder

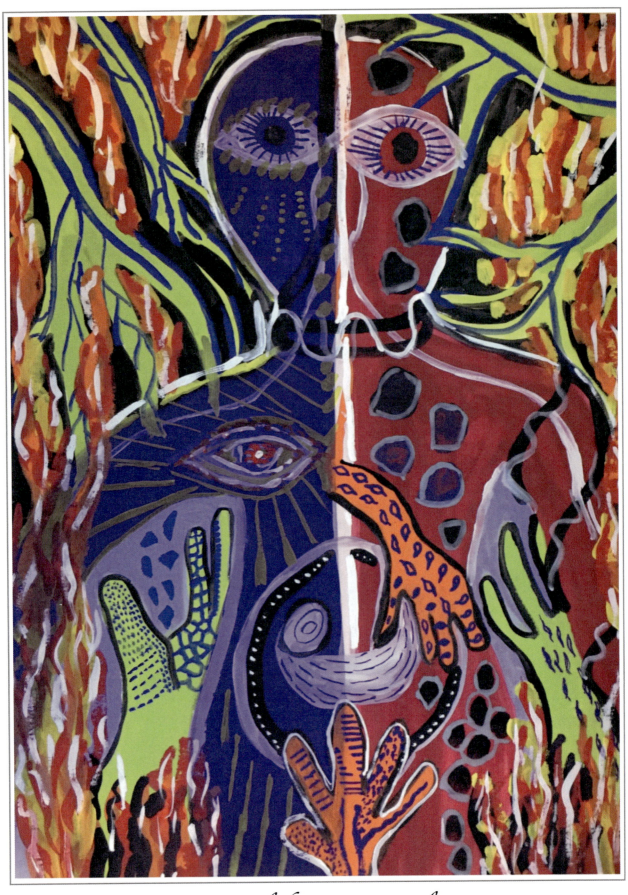

Untitled, Annette Walt

For Annette: Artist and Friend

Nitza Agam

Have I become the curator of your dreams?

Have I been able to witness your secret selves?

In your brightly colored paintings of your pain

In thickly taped portfolios?

They lay there for so many years stored in your attic

Full of torment, and beauty

I am sorry you had to hide them.

What do I do with them now?

Your art is part of the Museum of our long, loving, friendship with

All the milestones, all the joy and all the heartache.

I did not ask to be your curator.

I would rather you were alive.

I dream that you are still alive and instead of being sick

You are vibrant and your hair is streaked bright green

You live on in your hundreds of paintings and in my memory.

My wonderful, sweet, dear friend.

You live on in your art.

In Bloom

Barbara Greensweig

Giants, Fairies & Foxes—Oh My!

Leigh Verrill-Rhys

Storytelling is in my DNA.

I became aware of this proclivity at the age of three. I had awakened from a nightmare that I still remember. My father was asleep when I crawled into my parents' bed and snuggled between them. I told my father a story about a big round house I wanted him to build for me. The nightmare and the story had nothing in common, except perhaps the story was my way of dispelling the fear the nightmare instilled.

Stories are a human reaction to life's tribulations and uncertainties. From earliest times, humans have coped with terrors by relegating them to tall tales to entertain us around the campfire. A story shared is a fear conquered, an experience shared is one less trial to be faced alone or without knowledge.

My storytelling included tales I made up while I played alone in a grove of lilac bushes in the woods behind our house in Maine. I shared stories of actual experience when I started school after my family moved to California and had the opportunity to Show and Tell along with my first-grade classmates. On one occasion, I had ventured alone into Golden Gate Park and seen a fox. I described this sighting to my class. My teacher was skeptical and told my mother that I had an active "imagination"—which was certainly true, but the sighting was not imaginary.

My mother and siblings made fun of me about my "active imagination"—very little I said during this time was accepted as truthful. That alone kept me from expressing my thoughts and experiences to my family, so I began to "think" my stories while drawing my characters on newsprint paper with pencil and crayons.

Many months passed before I was vindicated by a television news report about foxes in the park. I had learned a lesson. I kept my stories safely to myself, fact, fiction or imagination.

A few years later, in fifth grade, our teacher assigned homework, encouraging her students to write a fairy tale—a completely imaginative story about an imaginary being. I sat at the table in our living room while my parents and siblings watched television and wrote a story about a giant. I now have no recollection of the story itself, only the experience of writing on lined paper with a green school pen that wrote with blue ink. I remember how excited I was to be able to write what my own imagination allowed me to conceive with the permission of my teacher.

Whether I received any plaudits or a good grade for my effort was and is irrelevant. I was free to tell a story. I was encouraged to use my imagination. Although I continued to think my stories as I drew my characters, that one opportunity was the catalyst for taking storytelling and writing seriously.

Another positive writing experience in education came when I was in ninth grade. The assigned reading was John Steinbeck's *The Red Pony* about which we were required to write an essay. My teacher at the time was Mr. Lombardi who was a treasure trove of excellent writing techniques, all of which I continue to implement.

My essay began with the statement, "Gitano was dead." Whatever followed has been lost in the many years that have passed, but I had made that statement as the most important fact I wanted to express and was also one of the writing treasures Mr. Lombardi shared with his class. When he returned my essay, the grade was written in red at the top: "A."

I had the assurance from a teacher whom I admired that I could, indeed, write well.

Because I enjoyed drawing while "thinking" my stories, I started college as an art student with ambitions to be a sculptor or painter or illustrator. I was soon shown the error of my ways and took a screenwriting class instead. As much as the idea of making films appealed, the fact remained I had an attachment to language and words on the page.

When I accepted that I painted pictures skillfully with words on a page or on a computer screen, that realization supported my decision to move from being an art student to become an English major with creative writing as the foundation.

My decision was not greeted with enthusiasm by my mother, but my stories were published in small, independent literary magazines, the creative writing department's own yearly publication, broadcast on a local NPR radio station. I won a writing contest and an award for my contribution to a national newspaper.

Yet, I resisted the call to take writing seriously enough. In 2008, came the event that set in stone what my resistance meant. A guest at a friend's 80th birthday party, asked my husband what he did. At first, he responded with a joke but eventually told the inquirer, "I'm a professional musician." The same person turned to me and asked what I did. I answered, "I've always wanted to be a writer." That admission embarrassed me to the core. So much so, that it changed my life.

I chose what I believed was the best of all the half-completed manuscripts I had amassed; worked, rewrote, polished, edited again, completed and submitted the first three chapters of the manuscript to an agent. The response eventually came: "My reader quite liked it." The agent requested the complete manuscript. I could say, "I'm a writer" at last. Months later, disappointment came but not before I had presented a proposal for another novel to a New York publishing company's editor at a writers' conference.

That synopsis was already on its way and another request for the full manuscript soon followed. Again, months passed. Late one December night, six months later, I received an email from the editor. "We would like to acquire *Wait a Lonely Lifetime*."

I skipped and trotted down the stairs into the kitchen. Bottle in hand, I swooped into the living room and asked my husband, "Is this the best champagne we have?" He knew instantly why I asked. As I had promised myself three years before that night, I have never said "I have always wanted to be a writer" again.

I am a writer. Although I don't make a living wage by writing, I have used my skill in all my paid employment and professional enterprises. I have been teased and insulted by friends; indulged by family and unquestioningly supported by my husband who never fails to ask, "Did you work on your new book today?" I claim "Writer" as my profession on all documents and questionnaires.

There is no other creative endeavor in which I release my creative spirit that gives me the satisfaction of achievement that writing a perfectly worded, and punctuated, sentence does. A day of work is neither complete nor satisfying without composing a few hundred words in paragraphs, pages, chapters of a book, an essay or a story.

To paraphrase Descartes, I write, therefore I am.

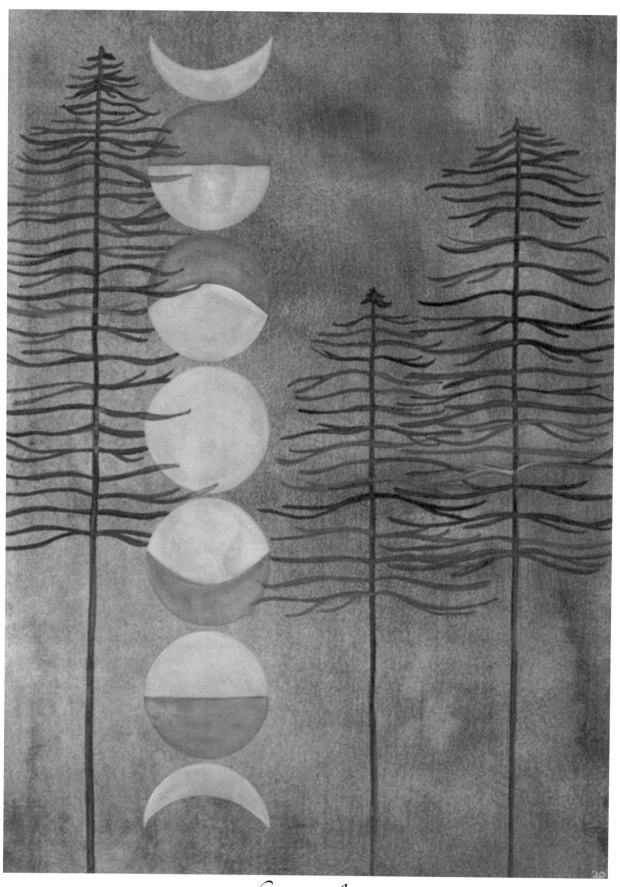

Moon Phases, Alison Trujillo

Annette's Garden

Marisa Handler

this is healing:
      wind rushing through
           right through me

mind of sky
      heart of sun
           limbs of earth
                water
                      my soul

sometimes an ocean
      sometimes a river
           at dawn
                a dewdrop

this is healing:
      a distilling—
           bee climbing into nasturtium
                snail coiling into shell

a growing small
      into this earthly body
           among these rustling chirping
                earthly bodies

a growing into
a slowing into
      the bodied firmament—
           O star-sung silence
                O amnesia's antidote
                      & alchemy's dream:

                the immortal coil

            ever the bud in the
      blooming and the
wilting

slowly now

slowly

    rocking

        and still:

            home.

San Miguel

Barbara Greensweig

Summer of 1972

Susan E. Light

Growing up in a middle-class Jewish family in Pittsburgh in the 1960s doesn't set a girl up for a scientific career. The family tree was laden with immigrant businessmen and housewives. The only woman physician I had ever met was a radiologist at the Children's Hospital when I had whacked my foot against the bathtub in our narrow bathroom in a futile attempt to exercise. Devoted to watching "Dr. Kildare" and "Ben Casey" (adoring the former and just tolerating the latter), I don't recall any women in medicine who weren't nurses.

The science classrooms at my high school were double the size of the regular classrooms to accommodate the labs. There were doors at both sides of the podium where Mr. Herman, the freshman biology teacher, stood passing out completed test papers as we shuffled out of the door of the first-floor classroom closest to the main entrance. As one of the younger teachers with a lawn mower haircut and a wide gap between his two front teeth, he had won the affection of his students with his sense of humor and direct style. He told us that he made as much money over the summer doing landscaping as he did teaching the remainder of the year. The message about what was important to him was clear, but his degree of honesty was unprecedented for that time and place. As he handed me my test paper, he looked me in the eye and said, "Good job."

At the top of the page, next to the 100% I had scored on the test, was a handwritten note:

Q: What does this mean?

A: That the test was too easy.

Shocked into silence more by the comment more than by the grade: was Mr. Herman saying that I was smarter than him? My comfortable position as a B student was now challenged. A rush of self-confidence passed through my body and that became the foundation for my future.

Caught between my inner drive, curiosity about the world outside my microcosm, and harboring society's expectations, my inner drive was taking the lead. By my junior year, my parents had heard enough of my scientific interest and causal comments about medical school that they sent me to the B'nai B'rith vocational counselor. Their real concern was a protective one: was I setting up unrealistic expectations for myself?

On a chilly and quiet Sunday morning in the winter of 1969, I went to his office above the Squirrel Hill News Stand and filled out all the multiple-choice questions. The following week my parents attended the session where the results were presented. His conclusion: "She's smart. She can do whatever she wants."

More importantly, he told me about how the National Science Foundation sponsored summer programs for high school students. My first serious rejection came when I wasn't accepted to the program at the Jackson Laboratory in Bar Harbor, ME, but did get into the program in biochemistry at the Loomis School in Windsor, CT. Not only did he reassure my parents about my ability to set my own goals, he showed me a path and a door that would lead me out of Pittsburgh.

Putting aside the Janis Joplin concert in New Haven, the weekend trips to New York City, going to Zabar's for the first time, staying with my roommate's family in Stuyvesant Town (and being amazed that you could have a supermarket on the block where you live) on the east side of Manhattan, that summer was about the science and culture. They gave this group of forty-eight rising high school seniors (thirty-two boys and sixteen girls, the proper ratio someone told the administration) the Lehninger's college biochemistry textbook. We went to lectures each morning and to our small research groups in the afternoon. My group was evaluating the effect of a choline deficient diet on lipoprotein accumulation in the brains of chicks. We sacrificed the chicks by beheading them and yes, chickens actually do run around with their heads cut off.

The life-changing component of the program was that although we had weekly tests each Saturday morning, they were corrected, but not graded. The program taught me that what was important was learning, not bringing home a grade to please one's parents.

The other important message that I took home that summer was that, in marked contrast to my life at home, it was okay to be a girl and like science. In high school, the boys were not interested in me, but rather in how I could help them with their homework. That summer was an almost level playing field and of greater influence than the thirty-two high school boys in the program were the male advanced students and instructors. Young men, who were entering and attending college, would interact with us as smart girls. Complementing that was the instructor of our research project, a smart energetic woman who was a student at Mt. Holyoke College. She was a valuable role model and always able to come up with a creative solution to the next problem as she hobbled around on crutches that summer.

We gathered in the lecture hall on July 20, 1969 to watch the moon landing. While the world saw our planet from a new vantage point, I now saw the world differently as well. There was a planet where my intellectual aspirations as well as my social agenda could coexist.

My interest in medical school waned after my summer at Loomis as I focused on basic science and contemplated graduate school. I returned the summer after my second year of college to be an instructor hoping to help a group of high school students experience what I had experienced a few years earlier.

A new director had been appointed for the program, and he lacked the warmth that Ed Ledbetter brought to the program three years earlier. His wife had a PhD, but she had chosen to not work and focus on the care of their young child. Having spent the previous summer doing organic chemistry research didn't prepare me for working on a project related to peptidoglycan in the cell membrane of *E. Coli*.

My group had a great rapport and the work was fun, but several weeks into the six-week program, I didn't think that we were making the progress I had expected. We couldn't even get standard growth curves for the *E. Coli*, and I shared my concern, frustration, and disappointment with the director in his office early one evening.

His reply was very direct and unforgettable: "That's why women shouldn't be in science." I froze and was speechless: I was asking for technical help, not career advice. All I was interested in was being a better instructor and teaching my students how to generate data to test a hypothesis. This wasn't the time or place to discuss his personal views. Since I was speechless, it was not difficult to gather my papers and quietly leave his office.

The punch line of the story is that at the end of the program my group did have some respectable data. I then learned that the four groups with male instructors who were working on parallel projects had also struggled, but didn't acknowledge it.

What I took away from the experience that summer was not that women shouldn't be in science, but that I needed to be very careful about when and where I would admit weakness and think carefully before asking for help. The director's remarks didn't deter me from my scientific goals, but opened my eyes to what I might expect to see as I continued on my journey.

The choice of medical school over a graduate program in biochemistry was guided by several parameters including my father's offer to pay for medical school (but not graduate school) and the landscape of the 1970s, where having a PhD did not promise a job offer. There was also the simple logic that going to graduate school meant I could do research while going to medical school would offer a choice between clinical medicine and research. In the end, I have done both.

Yes, I have asked for help along the way since asking for help, especially in a clinical setting, is the right thing to do.

I shared my story of "why women shouldn't be in science" at a talk to the winners of the science awards my daughter's high school a few years ago. There was an audible gasp from the audience, and for me it was a wonderful reminder of how things have changed. I was proof of that.

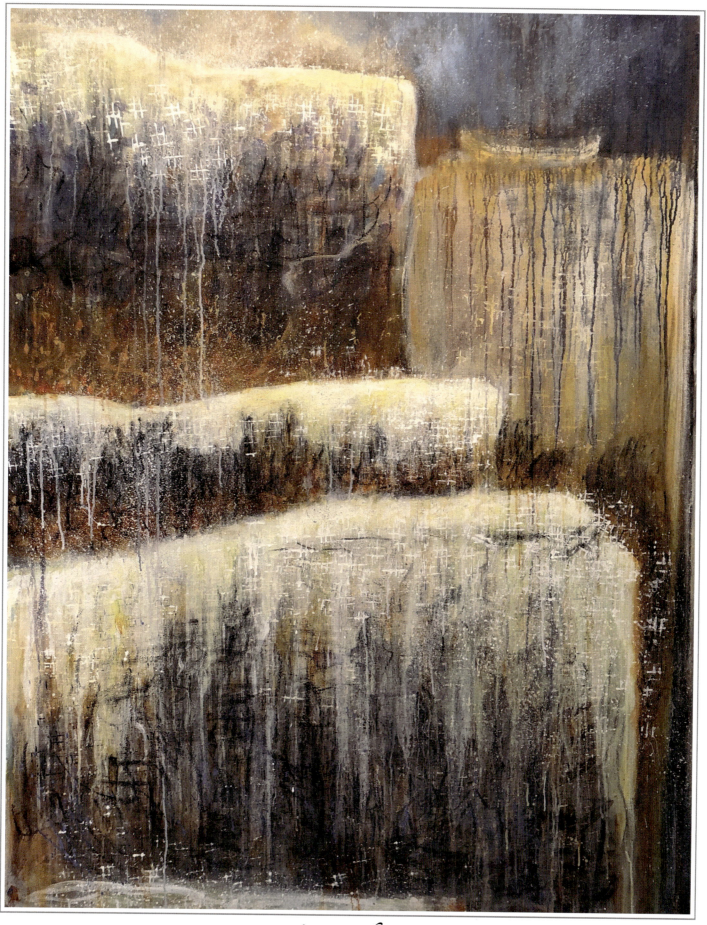

Boil, Jennifer Ewing

Half Moon at Dusk, Alison Trujillo

Poetry Medicine

Abby Caplin

I don't know when I became a poet.

I know I loved my seventh-grade journaling assignment and the feel of the soft pages as I sat on the beach at Oxnard, CA, watching my parents in their wet suits. They were out in the surf with their pitchforks, human sewing machines stitching their way along the wet sand, digging for Pismo clams. I was doing my homework, describing the long, cold beach, the dying light of the sunset, flies on the kelp, trying to ignore my frozen fingers and the incessant wind. I kept that journal for years, but now I can't find it anywhere.

Maybe it was when my eleventh-grade English teacher, Mr. Schoenman, had us read E.E. Cummings's "next to of course god america i." The poem was in line with the mood and teachings of the '60s, of politicians and the military industrial complex. When I began college, I told my mother I wanted to major in liberal arts, not science. She grew extremely upset and angry, demanding that I become a doctor. It was the feminist thing to do, she insisted. If her sons could be doctors, so could her daughter! I could write, do whatever I wanted, after medical school. I didn't have the courage to fight for my own path, since I wasn't sure what it was.

I convinced myself that I wanted to go into medicine. It seemed a worthy career, and I could travel. I could help people in small villages in Guatemala, or become a kibbutz doctor in Israel. But once you decide to become a doctor, the die is cast, and the timeline of your life is no longer yours. I'll list the steps here for my own review and your edification, to understand how I forgot myself:

First came a heavy load of undergraduate science courses, then studying for and taking the medical school entrance exam, going to interviews, moving to a new city, four years of medical school. Then came board exams and applying for licensure, applying and interviewing for three years of residency, during which I was on call in the hospital every third to fourth night. I'd arrive at the hospital at 7 a.m., spend the day constantly checking in on my patients, round on all the patients, admit new patients to the hospital, spend the night admitting and taking care of ward or intensive care patients. I was lucky to sleep an hour or two in the call room, rounding again in the morning on my patients, repeating more or less the same schedule until dinner, when I could finally drive home and collapse for twelve hours, just to start the cycle all over again.

After the three years of residency, I moved to San Francisco to complete two more years of specialty training, at which point life began to snowball: chronic illness, birth of a daughter, then a son, then my mother's death from cancer and onset of my father's Alzheimer's disease. It was easy to forget that I had ever wanted to write. I did have a few spurts of creativity, though. In 1986, after going to a medical convention in New Orleans, where drug companies handed out goody bags filled with pens, bottle openers, even oven mitts, I watched wealthy allergists scramble on the floor for the fake coins tossed by Mardi Gras performers, and was inspired to write a poem. I sent it to the Journal of the American Medical Association (JAMA), and of course, given my criticism of the medical establishment and level of skill, it was rejected. Another time, I was at a workshop for "recovering" doctors, and we were asked to write a poem in fifteen minutes. My poem was about a difficult friend who had just died of cancer, and in sharing it with the group, I found that I had reclaimed my writing self.

Years later I took an online poetry class, then continued to study privately with the poet Matthew Lippman, who had been one of my instructors. "How far do you want to take your poetry?" he asked me. "As far as I can," I said.

Though I've studied with many other teachers since and have published over a hundred poems to date, I know I'm still feeling my way into the poetry world. I wonder what might have happened had I bucked my mother, insisted I major in English, and moved in the direction that was truly mine to take. Maybe I would have written a few poems, gotten discouraged, and applied to medical school. Or maybe I'd be a famous poet. The only thing I know for sure—the poems would have been different because my life would have been different, and these days, I really wouldn't want to change a thing.

Limpet Nation 2

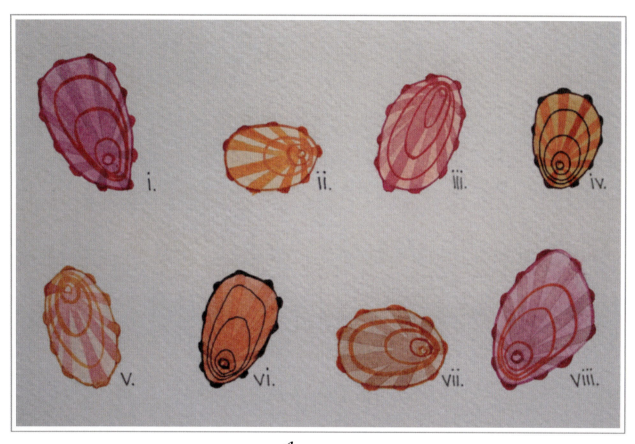

Alison Trujillo

Untitled, Annette Walt

Women's Work

Nitza Agam

As I was listening casually to NPR during a drive, a story caught my attention. It was about an elderly woman named Rita whose unfinished quilt had shown up in an estate sale. She'd passed away in her nineties without completing it. A woman artist who enjoys completing unfinished work purchased it. It was comprised of each state along with the state's symbol of the bird and the flag. Only in its beginning stages, the artist knew that the quilt would require a community of women to help finish it. Around the country, women responded to her invitation, signed on to the project, and worked together until it was completed.

The artist spoke about how women's projects so often remain unknown, whether they be art, journals, or incomplete manuscripts. How much do we have a responsibility to help those works continue, though the original artist could not? She may have given up or passed away before it could be shared. Completing women's unfinished artwork became this artist's mission, her way to support unique women so their work would no longer lie in drawers, hidden away for no one to see. It moved me.

I thought of my best friend who died a year ago, an artist who'd proudly created a collaborative women's quilt entitled "Twelve by Twelve." Each woman participating was responsible for twelve embroidered squares that were quilted together and shown at annual exhibits. Every year my friend proudly brought her twelve squares to my home to share with other friends and me. She'd place the squares on the floor, we'd gather around, and marvel at the colors and designs. I wanted to attend one of her annual quilt exhibits, but because of distance, I never made it. Now, in her memory, some of those squares hang on my wall.

But it is what my friend chose not to share or display that I now contemplate. Stacked in thick, taped, battered folders leaning against the wall in my office are hundreds of paintings she created during her years of art therapy in the 1980s where she allowed her uninhibited pain and vision to be expressed. With their rawness and intensity, and her focus on skeletons, fetuses, body parts and bright bold colors, they resemble Day of the Dead paintings influenced by artists such as Frida Kahlo.

She'd stored them in her attic, unknown and unseen, a trove of her soul hidden away in her intimate cottage, filled with art and nestled in lush gardens. These works were not on her wall and, like Rita's incomplete quilt, were never shared. Yet these paintings are completed pieces of art, colored in vibrant deep blues and reds, greens and orange, shades of purple and black. There are faces with thick black tears falling from their cheeks. The figure of a giant woman, like a hybrid of an octopus and skeleton, repeats through many of the paintings.

While she chose to display the more decorative art and her "Twelve by Twelve" quilt, these other deeply intimate, profound images of women trying to give birth, or expressing regret at not bearing children, stayed in her attic. Perhaps she'd had an abortion, or had been trying to figure out what role bearing children had in her life. She died childless, and while I assumed she may have had regrets, she seemed to relish her single life as an artist with a love of her home, two dogs, friends, and family.

These masterful paintings remain a mystery, with my office a virtual museum of her work. I've become the curator of these personal paintings revealing my friend's inner visions and longings. They are beautiful and compelling and deserve to be shown. She may not have intended them to be shared, but she also often repressed thinking of herself as an artist, fearing family censure. Art will not put food on the table, he'd tell her, prompting her to keep her work largely hidden. Hidden and unfinished works of art left by our treasured friends provide hope for the future of women's stories and artistic expression. How many other attics hide women's creative work? How much talent lies unfinished in estate sales or in refuse bins? How many women hide their work with shame, embarrassment, or fear? It's important to remember that if it were not for family members who found Emily Dickinson's poetry after she died, and decided to publish it, we might not have her poetry today.

I miss my friend, and hope she would encourage me to celebrate her artistry by bringing these bold, powerful paintings out of the dust and darkness into the light and the public eye. I will do so with pride and with love. I do it in her memory and in memory of women like Rita who could not complete her art, and all the women who felt compelled to hide their art in attics. Women's unfinished and hidden work deserves to be completed and shown. We replace fear and shame with hope and pride.

This essay was first published in Adanna Literary Journal, Issue No.10, 2020.

Half Moon Bay Nursery Interior

Barbara Greensweig

Friend Me

Marlene Shigekawa

It was in Silicon Valley in the mid-1980s, when high tech companies were booming, voices clashed and top dogs were rewarded, where I, a lone Asian woman manager, felt unheard. The drive to be heard found its way through my first published book—*Succeeding in High Tech: A Guide to Building Your Career*. It gave me an opportunity to prove myself as a writer and distinguish myself as a Japanese American woman. And in this situation, I felt compelled to "friend me," a term referring to the current Facebook technique, to overcome that alone feeling. I rewired my brain to use different parts of myself, to confront the two sides of me, the yellow face, and the white face, each with its separate Facebook page. Although my book was a nonfiction piece, I was able to fictionalize myself through the various characters I created who possessed a hard driving, people-person, entrepreneurial spirit, what I coined in my book a "mini-entrepreneur."

My bi-cultural upbringing as an all-American kid and a Japanese American paid off. Writing for me meant going undercover before emerging with ideas to be heard, for an Asian woman in the 1980s dominantly white male environment was not quite legitimate, an anomaly. My writing sparked my imagination to carve out a future as an Asian American creative artist while drawing from my rich and complex past. It was an extension of my childhood learning of how to operate in two cultures—mainstream American and Japanese American. It has been a lifelong journey of integration, finding ways to "friend me."

In the early 1980s, I entered the corporate world in San Francisco when the women's revolution began to take hold. Women could now get credit cards without using their husband's name. Companies were sued for job discrimination, and affirmative action practices reigned. When hiring me, a company could check two boxes —Asian and Woman—to fulfill legal employment laws. If you followed the advice in the trendy book, *Dress for Success*, you could almost be taken seriously. The buttoned blouse, hiding any speck of cleavage, the business suit, non-dazzling jewelry, and the power walk was the uniform of acceptability. This guidebook also suggested speaking "football" in corporate hallways and using phrases like "let him carry the ball" and "he's taking a long shot" to describe business practices. But it was not a ticket into the "ol' boys club." It was playing the right role, wearing the correct mask and being non-threatening to the white male ego. Often overlooked, I felt invisible in meetings with other managers when I was the only woman and minority in the conference room. I was the fly on the wall. To gain visibility, I wrote.

The qualities I ascribed to the characters in my book were those that went unrecognized in me, because my face erased any possibility of gaining recognition on the same level as a white male or female. So, I gained recognition by illuminating my successes through the accomplishments of others who were revered in their companies. I could be acknowledged for writing about successful people but could not earn the title for myself, a person who was like them in the flesh and capability but not in appearance.

How did I know this? When Americans were buying their Toyota and Honda cars in the 1980s, resulting in economic power in Japan, corporate America began looking at their competitor and replicating Japanese management practices, their "Quality Circles." As the Training Manager at a high-tech firm, I worked with a white male manager in charge of initiating Quality Circles. He made the comment to me, "Oh, you speak English so well." My silent, stifled reaction was: "Why wouldn't I? I'm an American, a third generation Asian American, not a recent immigrant, someone who has never visited Japan, and never learned to speak Japanese." Using my intuitive, cultural trigger of saving face, I merely said, "Thank you."

Although there was a feeling of underlying resentment and untapped seething rage, there also was a certain feeling of comfort, that at-home feeling of hiding my Japanese American sense of self that I had mastered by both listening to and watching my parents in the post-World War II era. After their lives were stripped away from them after the bombing of Pearl Harbor, they were exiled to a Japanese American incarceration camp in Arizona. They were forced to rebuild their lives after returning to California in 1945. Their resettlement took on a survival aspect of subservience and compliance after the trauma experienced from being denied their freedom as American citizens. I inherited this sense of being to some degree. Often feeling constrained, I didn't understand that my mother's warnings were meant to keep me safe. But her warnings didn't stop me from my daring teenage acts. We argued over wearing my skintight capri pants that showed off my sexually inviting butt.

A high school English teacher blabbed to my mother that I was making out in the hallway with my white boyfriend. My mother often posed the question following my overly bold behavior: "What will people think?" I was bringing shame on my family. But, later as I grew into adulthood, my mother did question whether my out-of-classroom behavior was tied to my low grades in English class. Now I see that this tight teeter-totter of moving between compliance and rebellion is a gift. It enables me to be not only bicultural, but it deepens my understanding of nuances, my understanding of the meaning behind the real meaning, and the ability to recognize how prejudice is packaged, sold, and, sometimes, unknowingly perpetuated.

For my mother, acceptance in our all-white community in Southern California translated into: "You have to be better than anyone else." In other words, we had to be twice as good in order to be considered equal to our white counterparts. There were also warnings to avoid bringing attention to ourselves, to stay out of the sun so as not to become too dark. I ignored her warnings and enjoyed spring break with my white girlfriends by going to the beach, basking in the sun, and acquiring a dark tan. I was the only one with my olive skin who didn't smear on tons of suntan lotion. Now I understand that her underlying fear was associated with the evacuation and imprisonment of 120,000 Japanese Americans and herself. My existence demanded straddling two cultures—mainstream American and Japanese American—and overcoming the chains of oppression.

But I was often confused. My mother's desire to be seen as more American than Japanese to our white community signaled that it's dangerous to openly show our Japanese culture. We would eat Japanese cuisine about once a month. On one occasion, our family was eating our Japanese meal with chopsticks. We looked out the window and noticed that our white neighbors were coming to visit us. My mother quickly took the chopsticks and other dishes and dashed with them to the kitchen sink to hide them. Her survival skills were once again triggered. I observed this odd behavior and concluded that my Japanese side was to be kept hidden, out of sight to all those non-Japanese.

It wasn't until I traveled to Japan for the first time when I was forty-five years old that I began to feel whole. It felt like being with relatives. Those Japanese words occasionally spoken by my parents rang true there. Words expressed by our Japanese taxi driver gave validation to what I heard at home in America. As I mingled among other Japanese women at the bathhouse and observed their lithe bodies, I was freed from feeling shameful of my own body. I no longer felt the need to hide my body as I did in my seventh-grade gym class when taking a shower among my white classmates.

And this betwixt between position, of straddling two cultures, has enabled me to artfully create acts of defiance in the form of writing books, creating film scripts, and producing films, in which the heroes and heroines are Japanese American. My first documentary film, *For the Sake of the Children*, unleashes the long-suppressed voices of intergenerational trauma experienced by four generations of Japanese Americans. It was a work that was meant to express gratitude to my parents and all our Japanese American ancestors who were imprisoned and were able to surmount adversity. My creative work has helped to make a shift, not only for me, but for others from being a victim to becoming a superhero, without the masquerade or superpowers, the feeling of being empowered. I no longer seek the approval of "Friend Me," for I now equally appreciate both cultures.

Sparkle, Jennifer Ewing

My Death According to Poetry

Doreen Stock

My death according to Poetry

leaves me with one arm

already among the angels

its wing pointing earthward

in a sweep of the grey clouds

threatening five valleys

with cold water

My death according to

Poetry leaves me with

one hand clutching

the purse I was given

by my mother

in it a sandwich

I have been eating now for years . . .

The salmon that swam into that

sandwich suffered its way

onto a singular hook

and was clubbed over the head.

My death according to Poetry

is printed in pages

of red and white checked oilcloth

that crack

in the center

and will never be published.

There are songs I never sang

according to Poetry

But Poetry lies.

Bella Luna, Gretchen Butler

A Love Story

Darshell McAlpine

I didn't know I wanted to do this always until I did this. Until the streams of combustible conflagration held up in my consciousness burned through my fear, coursing through the pen pressed tightly between my fingertips. Until the universe whispered her secrets in my ears soliciting me to gossip. Until I found the courage to disrobe letter by letter. Until I believed the comeliness of my elocution. Until the words made me real.

There is a current of desperation that is ever-present when you grow up in certain environments. We lived in a lot of places, but it's life in the projects I absorbed most. Even as a child, I felt the desperation though I lacked the words to articulate it. I carried a book everywhere with the hopes there would be time for me to escape into it. I guess you could say my longing to be extricated from the desperation birthed my first stories.

Throughout elementary and middle school, my penchant for words alienated me from many of my peers.

Why do you talk like that?

Why do you use all those big words?

You're trying to act white?

You think you're so smart?

I hid myself in books where the words embraced and intrigued me without castigation. So, I gathered them to myself, pondering their form, how they began from one letter to become entire thoughts. How can the seemingly insignificant "a" combine with other seemingly insignificant scribble to create glorious expressions? Could I harness this power? Was it possible I could make the words do what I wanted them to, just like those whose books transported me all over the world and to the farthest galaxies? Could I make the words mine?

Writing did not flinch at my inexperience. It became a way I could say what I felt needed to be said without drawing attention to myself. Words permitted me to shed my skin, to build entire worlds only I could control. My writing crafted a perfect safe space, a dwelling for my soul, where I could be unabashedly me. I could embellish or be truthful, play the villain or the heroine, create characters and annihilate them. Whether it was short fiction or pontificating essays, writing allowed me to become the master of my existence.

When I worked up the bravery to share my words as a child, I was ridiculed. Told I was too intelligent or too curious for a black girl from the projects, too ambitious, too sagacious, too impoverished, too broken. I absorbed the mockery and believed those words for a time, going so far as to live them out. Words have power, but if you are a writer, then you know the words long to become stories and the stories will not allow you to rest until they are told. The storyteller in you will torment you until she is satisfied.

> *"Why am I compelled to write? . . . Because the world I create in the writing compensates for what the real world does not give me. By writing I put order in the world, give it a handle so I can grasp it . . . To convince myself that I am worthy and that what I have to say is not a pile of shit . . . I write because I'm scared of writing, but I'm more scared of not writing."—Gloria E. Anzaldúa*

In high school, the universe saw fit to bless me with Sarah Bennett and Virginia Havens, my English teachers. They were both staggeringly difficult, anaphylactic if exposed to poorly constructed prose. Each was merciless in her critiques. It was Mrs. Bennett who made certain I would not continue to misspell the word occasion by reminding me that adding an extra "s" to the word (occassion) made an ass of the writer. Mrs. Havens stood in front of my desk with her hands on her knees, just so we were eye to eye as she told me the essay I had recently submitted was trivial and beneath me. Neither would allow me to be mediocre as a writer. They both shared their belief with me that I could do dramatically more with my writing. Their instruction and encouragement restored my confidence in my ability, and I am forever grateful to them for changing the way I connect with language.

Letters strung together to form words strung together to form ideas strung together to become narratives are intoxicating. Writing is as much a passion as it is an addiction, but committing to my writing is one of the most difficult things I've done. Despite my love affair with words, I have not always been a faithful lover. I have allowed any and everything to come between me and my love. As I pen these words, I am excited, full of adrenaline, eagerly anticipating the finished product, lovingly massaging the text to communicate eloquently and effectively. And yet, despite the euphoria they give me, sometimes I refuse to engage with the words.

Opposite the excitement of writing, and just as profound, is the anguish that comes from it. So if I'm not ignoring or avoiding my writing, I am ruminating over it like a school-aged child stuck on a problem with the simplicity of $1 + 1 = 2$. I write and rewrite and rewrite and discard and start over and painstakingly finish and edit, reedit and have it edited, until I have whack-a-moled my neuroses enough to press the publish button. Seldom is it good enough, and there are always a bunch of things I wish I had said or didn't say. I cannot escape the idea that every piece could be better. Then I read Toni Morrison's *The Bluest Eye* or listen to Neil Gaiman and Margaret Atwood's masterclasses and want to scrap everything I've written and start over. Their writing is rhythmic, emotional, deliberate, and captivating. I want to provoke in my readers what these authors provoke in me.

With each word I write, I am chasing moments of literary exultation. The exhilaration of a well-crafted sentence, phrase, idea, article, blog, book, is what constrains me to keep at it. When conjured, the words come from some deep faraway place inside of me. A place I only glimpse when I am not trying so hard. When the current of the love for what I am doing overtakes me, carrying me where it wills. I am powerless to fight against it, and why would I? Right in this place, I am overwhelmed with so much emotion that sometimes tears and laughter flow together. When I am here, I write for no other reason than the absolute joy of it. I have no plans to get rich or famous. I need no accolades. Perfection can't breathe at this altitude. I see my own words on the page and simply marvel at how bare I am, excited to climb and unafraid to fall. I write because I can . . . I can.

Autumn Afternoon

Barbara Greensweig

The Balancing Act

Barbara Greensweig

I grew up in a traditional Jewish home where women were expected to become teachers or nurses and art—although strongly encouraged by my parents—was ultimately seen as a frivolous endeavor, an addendum to one's life, not the core. The idea of attending an art academy never was considered by me, and I attended a university and became a teacher of English and art, married young and, by the age of thirty-two, had three children. My husband was the main breadwinner; I stayed at home to raise children. My ability to create was relegated to after the children were asleep; I would paint in a corner of my bedroom often until two in the morning. My life as an artist became a balancing act between practicality and creativity, heightened by the fact I was a woman.

My children—and now my grandchildren—are certainly the best creations I have ever had a hand in making. I have been fortunate to have a husband who supports my artistic endeavors. Yet I have always felt the tug between the practicalities of life—the duties of a faithful wife and mother—and the desire to create. This attitude may reflect my generation, that marriage and children take precedence as they surely should, but how does one also find the time to discover oneself? How do you find the time to paint? —a commonly asked question over the years. I don't. I make the time to paint because it is a core to who I am.

From the time I was presented with a birthday gift of quality art supplies at age eight, the need to create became crucial to my being. As a child, I would hide my paintings in my closet or under my bed because I didn't think they were good enough for others to see. I fortunately had parents who thought anything I did was wonderful and would discover, what to them were hidden treasures, and frame them. It took me years to describe myself not simply as an artist but as a "professional artist." I use this term to communicate to people that what I do is not a whim, but something I take seriously, and something I want them to take seriously. Let me relate one story that was a turning point for me. Children talk about what their parents "do"; my son would tell his friends that his mother is an artist. One day my son was at the house showing his friend my studio, and his friend said: "Wow, your mom REALLY is an artist." Somehow that statement by a youngster became a turning point for me. I began to respect my own ability to do art.

As I teetered on a balancing scale between family life and being an artist, I quickly discovered the role that finance plays into the equation. Artists are predominantly judged and validated by their sales. The more money a work of art fetches, the more successful must be the painting and the artist who did it. Any art show I have ever done has prompted the same question from friends and family: How were your sales? This is a matter of practicality—sales generate money and artists need to support themselves—but is art valid for art's sake? The answer obviously should be yes. But the dilemma to create salable paintings—subject matter that appeals to the masses and will sell versus art for art's sake—will always be a continual struggle for an artist. If sales are not there, and unsold art accumulates, then the balancing scale tips away from creativity.

How does one become an artist while trying to run the traditional family life of raising children, carpooling, cooking, laundry, walking the dog, paying bills, and all the mundane aspects of existence? I validated myself by having a studio built behind my home, a place in which to paint, to hang my paintings, to do art shows. It takes great courage to hang a painting on a wall, to say to the public, "This is good enough to go in your home," that my experience in painting deserves to be shared and seen by others. One must be brave enough to admit to oneself that every painting one does will be better than the previous one, that by parting with this work of art, I will be spurred on to create something of a higher quality. Ultimately, my hope is that the joy I feel when creating a painting can resonate with the viewer and create joy in the new space where it will be hung. I will have paintings that never sell. Those will remain with me. Perhaps they are my art for art's sake.

I have spent six decades creating art that captures to me moments in time. The subject matter of my work is connected with the places I visit and the geographic locations where I have lived. I began painting lavender fields and sunflowers in France before either became trendy. I visited colonial Mexico numerous times and painted the vibrant adobes and cascading flowers. I have been lucky to have lived close to vineyards in Sonoma County, and later by the coast in Northern California. Painting is a way I can communicate my experiences so that the viewer can relive those special feelings of time and place. When the connection resonates between artist and viewer, then a work of art truly has soul. During the pandemic of 2020, I received an email one day from a woman who had purchased several paintings over the years. She wanted me to know that as she sheltered in place in her home, she passed by my paintings each day and they brought joy into her life. And I thought to myself—this is what art is all about and why I do what I do.

My life is still a balancing act of family responsibilities versus making time to create. Once a week I carve out several hours to paint on location, to find the beauty in the world as I commune with nature. My studio always has an open door inviting me to enter. Sales are not as important as they used to be. I am happy to paint what I choose. I find the subject matter that speaks to me. I still take great joy in what I do, and am happy when I get notes from others telling me that my paintings have continued to bring them joy. My story is not unique. It is a story shared by many women from my generation and before, but also probably going forward as well. My art is no longer relegated to the corner of my bedroom nor stashed in hidden places. I had a dream to do art and I never gave up on that dream. I can balance my life and be a wife, mother, grandmother, and yes, an artist too.

Golden Bird, Gretchen Butler

Stories and Moving Pictures

Marlene Shigekawa

When I was six, I would watch my mother drive our 1949 blue and gray Chevy, observe how she would shift the gears and step on the clutch. I would memorize every movement so that when I grew up, I could drive my car like she did and alone go to a field or the beach and take my easel and paint the surrounding landscape or seascape. I wanted to be an artist.

When entering my elementary school cafeteria for lunch, I was surprised to see my drawing made from colored crayons hanging with other drawings. There, on the wall was one drawing from each class. I remember drawing myself near the chicken coop where I would be feeding the chickens. Of course, in my creation there was the obligatory elementary school image of a sunburst in the upper right-hand corner, myself dressed in the yellow and brown polka-dot dress my mother had made and my black hair in pigtails. My mother always made sure that I was color coordinated. Yellow ribbons were tied to the end of my pigtails. Another time, when driving home from school with my mother, I saw giant red strawberries with faces adorning the windows of Curry's ice cream shop. The following week, my drawing of giant red strawberries not only with faces but dancing legs greeted all that entered the cafeteria.

Why were my drawings displayed on the cafeteria wall not just one week but several? The pictures I had in my head traveled from me to that display wall where other eyes could see them. There was this black-haired girl appearing on the wall where many blond-haired, blue-eyed classmates could see her. My imagination, how I saw my world, was shared and I was surprised. I think I gained some confidence in feeling that what I imagined was something special to share. But why would anyone want to know about me?

I discovered that what I wanted to say, to write about, my perspectives were meaningful, but I was not the right person to share them. While in college, I wrote an essay titled *Freedom is Slavery* that caught the eye of the student editor of our college publication. But I quickly learned from the faculty advisor that when readers saw my name they would think of the "South Seas," an Asian person, and that nobody would believe I wrote the essay. My article was not published. I encountered the same reaction when told by a university professor that he doubted I wrote my beautifully written essay on Lord Byron's poetry. My need to be accepted stifled my need to become outraged. My rage did not come until later.

My divorce was a painful gift that prompted me to explore what I really wanted to do with my life. I became aware that I wanted to become a film director. The stories and the pictures that I was compelled to tell were associated with shame and unspoken family pain and humiliation, surrounding the Japanese American incarceration experience. My mother, five months pregnant with my brother, exiled from vibrant Southern California to the hot, desolate Arizona desert, told of how she got off the train, and was forced to drink water filled with mud. The pain, humiliation, and rage were there, hiding just underneath the surface, now bubbling over.

My initial creations were children's picture books. I asked my favorite uncle to do the illustrations to accompany my stories, family stories I heard as a child. I allowed my shiny wooden blue jay, crafted by my maternal grandfather in the incarceration camp, to take flight in my first children's book, *Blue Jay in the Desert*. It led to numerous book readings. Wide-eyed students listened and stared in disbelief at my grandfather's carved blue jay pinned to my chest, triggering insightful questions. White teachers expressed their gratitude for stories that had been kept hidden away for years. Japanese American audiences relived the pain, leading to validation and some healing. My legacy was linked to their legacy. I still couldn't quite fathom that my creation with my uncle could have such an impact, that others were moved from a simple act of telling a story using pictures. I realized that my healing had become healing for others in processing collective/community pain. Then I remembered the messages I had received in college.

I have now shifted from the printed story to moving picture stories or films. So, my goal of becoming a counselor/therapist has shifted from a treatment office to the film screen. I never thought that I would become a documentary filmmaker. *For the*

Sake of the Children captures the voices of not only those imprisoned but the voices of their children and grandchildren. Again, I was surprised but grateful that audiences were moved to a collective healing experience.

With all of this, I have traveled from feeling ashamed of my Japanese American background to feeling proud, finding strength from my family survivors, moving from being private to having a public persona. Then I remember my drawing, which was displayed in my school cafeteria. That sunburst in the corner now takes center stage, shining brightly. At the same time, I continue to struggle and feel the conflict of wanting to be accepted and wanting to speak out and be an advocate, of fighting prejudice and seeking social justice. It is a lifelong struggle that fuels me to create.

Holy Water, The Ganges, Varanasi, India

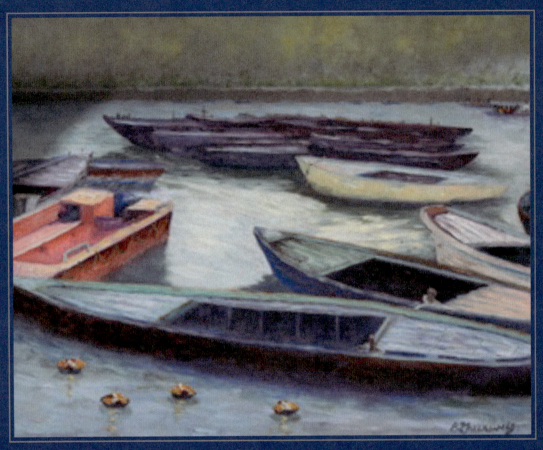

Barbara Greensweig

Sake of the Children captures the voices of not only those imprisoned but the voices of their children and grandchildren. Again, I was surprised but grateful that audiences were moved to a collective healing experience.

With all of this, I have traveled from feeling ashamed of my Japanese American background to feeling proud, finding strength from my family survivors, moving from being private to having a public persona. Then I remember my drawing, which was displayed in my school cafeteria. That sunburst in the corner now takes center stage, shining brightly. At the same time, I continue to struggle and feel the conflict of wanting to be accepted and wanting to speak out and be an advocate, of fighting prejudice and seeking social justice. It is a lifelong struggle that fuels me to create.

Holy Water, The Ganges, Varanasi, India

Barbara Greensweig

Thoughts on Being an Asian American Woman Writer...

Cynthia Chin-Lee

1934 Baltimore, MD.

Someone was knocking on the door.

Then seven years old, Nancy was folding clean diapers for her mother, but her father grabbed her arm and shoved her into the closet. Her father warned, "Get in there and be quiet!" He then calmly proceeded to open the front door and chat with the local truant officer. The officer's eyes narrowed as he said, "We heard you have a school-age child? She should be attending school. That's the law." Nancy's father invited the officer to look around the house. Only small children were playing in the backyard, all too young to go to school. While Nancy should have been going to school, she was held back so she could help take care of her younger siblings. She was not allowed to attend school until her brother, a year and a half younger, was old enough to go to school. By that time, it would be useful to have her walk with him as her parents cared about educating him, but not her.

Nancy was my mother, a talented visual artist and a wonderful storyteller. Though she had won a prestigious state-wide art contest when she was twelve, she didn't have the opportunity to showcase her talent. When she graduated high school, her parents demanded she stay home and work in the family restaurant even after she won a two-year scholarship to the Corcoran School of Art in Washington, D.C. They told her she'd have to turn it down and support her younger brother's ambition to attend college. Luckily Nancy had a teacher who mentored her and got the school to give her a one-year scholarship. Her parents reluctantly accepted. Unlike my mother, I never had to worry about getting an education because my parents encouraged, nagged, and reminded me I would go to college and have a career. As a young kid, I loved words. I read voraciously and wrote in a diary about the ups and downs of life, my observations of the school yard, the family, and the hurts and crushes of youth. I also noted the snub of classmates who looked down on and intentionally excluded the Chinese girl, the taunt of bullies, and the seemingly innocent remarks from neighbors.

I write for many reasons: free psychotherapy, venting my outrage at social injustice, racism, sexism, and the drive for self-expression. When I was five or six, I remember my tow-headed neighbor, Cathy, asking me why I had black hair. She couldn't understand why I looked different, and I didn't know what to say. At seven years old, my brother and I were playing at the park on a Saturday afternoon when a boy with a crew cut and a mean throw took a bucket of water balloons and started pelting us, chanting, "Ching Chong Chinaman."

My parents told us when they first looked for our home in the Chevy Chase area of Washington, D.C., the real estate agent told them they would have to get permission from the neighbors. Chinese families just couldn't buy a house in that neighborhood even if they had the money. There were clauses in the contracts; no Orientals or people of Mongolian descent could buy there, but maybe the neighbors would turn a blind eye. Fortunately, they did and we loved our tree-lined block and our roomy house complete with basement and attic, walking distance to the elementary school.

When I was eight years old, my oldest brother, Bruce, was eighteen and getting ready for college. He took a job at McDonalds in Bethesda, Maryland. Because he'd have to take two or three buses to get there, my uncle Edmond loaned him his MG roadster. Bruce drove the sporty MG to his job filling ketchup canisters and became the target of racist coworkers. They didn't like his fancy car or his future college education. One weekend, when my parents were on a rare holiday in New York, Bruce shook me awake in the middle of the night. *What in the world?* Groggily, I got up and stumbled to a window overlooking the back of the house; the MG was engulfed in flames, a firetruck's yellow lights flashed over and over in the blackness. Bruce pulled me from the window and hustled me out the front door away from the fire. The next day, we sadly looked at what was left of the shell of the car. I could crumble the glass window in my fingers, and I stroked the rough bark of the magnolia tree that didn't survive the fire. I found out our neighbors had seen the fire and called the fire station for us and then called to wake us up. We suspected arson, but as far as I know, the fire was never investigated.

Two years later, my parents took us to the city records office for a special event. We were changing our last name from Chin to Chin-Lee. Chin was our paper name, the name my grandfather used when he immigrated to the United States from China. It wasn't his real name. Chinese people weren't allowed to immigrate to the United States from 1882 with the passage of the Chinese Exclusion Act until its repeal in 1943. The act was overturned because the U.S. became an ally of China during World War II.

From the 1880s until then while English, Irish, French, Italians, Germans, and other white people freely came to the country in the tens of thousands, California Senator Leland Stanford helped pass the act that barred Chinese from coming to the country. The Chinese were forced into ghettos, lynched, and often criminalized. A small quota of a few hundred Chinese could enter the country legally as merchants, diplomats, or students.

My grandfather bought the papers of a Chinese person who had been in the U.S. legally; my grandparents pretended to be the people on these papers. A "paper" son, my grandfather and his wife, my grandmother, had to memorize all the details of their papers, and they would live in the U.S. under this pretense for decades. Fortunately, both my parents were born in the U.S. and automatically became U.S. citizens. As my grandfather reached his 80s, he asked my father to return to the clan name, Lee, and my father agreed.

By that time my father was already in his 40s and had a thriving medical practice in Washington, D.C.'s Chinatown. It would have been confusing for his patients had he gone from Dr. Chin to Dr. Lee. Somehow, Dr. Chin-Lee was close enough to Dr. Chin that most people could make the adjustment. My dad honored my grandfather's wish by making Chin-Lee our legal last name, reminding us daily of our country's harsh immigration laws and treatment of people of color, particularly non-assimilable Asians.

Despite my background, I recognize that I grew up with many advantages, daughter of a medical doctor and Ivy League education. Those advantages have helped me become a writer. As a writer, I'd like to share the stories of my community and others who don't fit in. I believe the point of literature is hope. If others can overcome adversity, then maybe we can, too. Because I write from the pain of exclusion, I want my books to be inclusive. Because I often felt like I didn't belong, I want to welcome and embrace the outsider.

The Space Between Us

Barbara Greensweig

Lemon Tree, Avigile Gottlieb

The Lemon Tree

Nitza Agam

I stopped eating. I had forgotten the effects of extreme anxiety. The last time I stopped eating was during the 1973 Yom Kippur War in Israel. I was living with my boyfriend when a siren sounded and he got into his army uniform, put an apple and a toothbrush in his army duffel bag, and left to join his unit. A week later he was killed. During that week I stopped eating too. Then I lost almost twenty pounds; this time, it was more like eight. The coronavirus pandemic reminded me of living through a war. The lockdown in San Francisco was like that siren. Life changed dramatically that moment. It would not be the same. Now the enemy was invisible, and I was not sitting in an underground bunker worried about bombs or the fate of my boyfriend, but I was at home in what would become my fortress with family and a disabled husband in a wheelchair.

That first week I was so scared that one of us would get the virus. What would I do? My husband depended on me for everything. He might not make it through the virus, and if I got it, he didn't have the help he needed, and we could not call on friends or family to help. It seemed like an impossible scenario. I found familiar tools that I had forgotten about as well. Just like I had forgotten what life-threatening anxiety and uncertainty felt like, I had forgotten what could help ease it. I found yoga classes online and my body relaxed; my mind was able to let go of the knots, the thoughts, the fear. Once upon a time in my youth, I had practiced yoga but had let it go. Now it returned and the voice of the young yoga teacher became my lifeline.

As time moved on, the fear of getting the virus diminished. I established the routine of our life, our morning chores and tasks, a walk in the neighborhood, conversations with friends, with my therapist. I realized that childhood trauma played a role in the fear. When I was three years old, I got whooping cough and was enveloped in an oxygen tent. That might explain my lifelong claustrophobia. I could not imagine being intubated or secluded. The three-year-old who wanted her mother and out of that enclosure emerged as did the twenty-two-year-old survivor of war and loss. I was both.

I took comfort in the lush, green lemon tree outside our window near our veranda. It became an altar as I faced it every morning doing yoga or my own kind of prayer. I loved watching it change in the light. I picked lemons in the evening inhaling the scent, grateful for each day, each morning that we were healthy. I enjoyed watching the neighbor's ginger cat stretching out in our backyard, the variety of birds flitting from branch to branch.

Sometimes I saw "Ginger" climb over walls and fences under clouds and green hills behind him. I learned to cherish those small moments more than ever. I was the three-year-old wanting her mother, the twenty-two-year-old fearful for the safety of her fiancé during a war. Yet I was now the sixty-nine-year-old safe in the refuge of my home, hoping for the best. Along with the rest of the world, I sought sanctuary. I made the ordinary spaces more sacred, as I hid from the virus, and slowly overcame my fear.

Limpet Nation 1

Alison Trujillo

Ice Canyon

Jennifer Ewing

How Art Has Made All the Difference

Jennifer Ewing

What would I be if I were not an artist? For this mostly right-brained human, the answer might have led to great unhappiness. I am not a linear thinker nor do I like to be boxed in. Freedom for me and my creative spirit is what keeps me going.

Over the years I have wondered if only I had more of a musical ear or a scientific interest, what might have happened to my path? Now in my early seventies, I can look back on this question a bit more objectively and less passionately than in earlier decades. So much water under the bridge that this question does not intrigue me as it used to. So much has happened to confirm the success of my childhood decision to be an artist. I am very much at home with my chosen path and am grateful for what this has given me and all that I have been able to share. Art seems to whisper in my ear as a muse would do in ancient times. This soft voice gives me insights into my potential and helps me go further.

When I was seven, my mother tried to get me into other pursuits that failed miserably. Like ballet, where I was in agony most of the time. When the class ended we were required to put on a pageant with real ballet outfits and a very scary audience that traumatized me. Tap dancing was marginally better than ballet, but I was not graceful nor coordinated. And again, there was a final big pageant full of judging eyes to endure. Dancing for me was a foreign land that I wanted to stay far away from. And I had not an ounce of affinity for that art form.

Piano lessons lasted longer and were more brutal because there was always that ugly old piano sitting in the living room just waiting for me to tend to my practice. My mother would beg me to play for company, and that became a consistent torture. She loved to play the piano so of course, I would too. The good side was that my younger sister had to go through all this with me, and we could commiserate.

My father tried his best to make me into a mathematician at a very early age. This was his passion, and he had some good tricks up his sleeve which still bring a smile to my face. He would make a "fun" set of flash cards and use them as if they held magic powers. His reverence for numbers and sequences were not passed down to his daughters. His second love was chess, and he played whenever he could. We always had a chessboard close by that my sister and I avoided like the plague. I believe that math and chess have their very own language that I could never learn or speak nor cared about. I had found another one.

I begged for art lessons. At least my grandfather recognized my fledgling abilities and talked my parents into sending me off to the Chicago Art Institute for classes. This provided a whole new world for me to explore in a very cool place that was ten L stops away from my house. I loved riding the L and walking into the Institute. It was far greater than school or even church for me. It was an exotic art palace where I would be encouraged to try out my drawing and painting skills in the midst of huge collections of masterworks. All those paintings in frames made me dizzy with energy that fed my soul.

My grandfather, Curt Behm, came from a family of wood carvers who had immigrated from Germany. He had grown up surrounded by massive furniture crafted with exceptional skill. His appreciation for art was high, and this filtered into my curious childhood brain. He was no stranger to the Art Institute because his father, Gustav, had taught wood carving there in 1900, and Curt had great respect for the school.

In the 50s there was a contest one could find on the inside of a matchbook where a prize was offered for duplicating a man's profile printed there. I seem to remember that the man had a hat and had a pipe. This gave him character. The reward was a scholarship for drawing lessons. My grandparents would prompt me multiple times to try my hand at this. It was fun and I felt a kind of calling from a larger world far outside my house. But I never remember entering the contest. Another pause to question what might have been.

When I was seven, I would accompany my father downtown to his chess club where one chess player was also an artist. His name was Jules Stein, and I will always be grateful for how he demonstrated to me the way contour lines worked to achieve a likeness by a deft and confident hand. I was mesmerized as I imitated his lines and became more confident myself. It felt so empowering to be able to draw with ease like Jules. He also taught me an appreciation of how chess players usually sit very still which is key to getting an accurate likeness.

After seventh grade, nothing else mattered to me but art. Drawing became my superpower—a way to see and listen to the world with some degree of mastery in my back pocket. It was the most rewarding of all my activities for I could measure my progress in an easy way. The results were there on paper or canvas and I loved seeing my sketchbooks fill up. When I drew or painted I was lost into another state that transported me far away from my parents' squabbles or the pressure to perform in other subjects. I learned early that art was transformational and challenging and had made a huge difference in other artists' lives.

At the Art Institute, we heard stories of artists and how the creative spirit worked for them. Today, I am still enchanted by the act of drawing and painting. It is my unique voice as much as the way I speak. The inner excitement of capturing a feeling or a gesture has never left me. It has made all the difference in how I have lived my life and has showed up in the choices I have made for work.

I began my career as an elementary art teacher, then an illustrator, a drawing instructor for a junior college and later a graphic artist for engineering firms. In 1988, I married Leo, and on our extended honeymoon, we delighted in great Italian fresco cycles. On return, I broke from the corporate world and opened my own mural painting business. The big reasons were freedom and a longing to explore color on a large scale like those magical fresco paintings. I took a big chance for I had no real business experience—simply faith that this could work.

In 2009, I started an evening program at the deYoung Museum, where I was working as a teaching artist in the daytime. For a few short years, this was heaven for me, teaching adults who wanted a dive into the world of drawing. It was full circle since I was back in the museum world again. Familiar territory that felt like home.

My current body of work is dedicated in honor of my father, Paul Ewing. When my father died, my new art form, *Spirit Boats,* was born. In using the Spirit Boat, I transitioned from grief to an ongoing celebration of life. I found a new way to express my inner world and in turn work with people. The Spirit Boat is a multicultural and universal symbol of movement—a sacred vessel that helps one access the unseen world and navigate life with metaphysical support. In my paintings, drawings, sculptures, installations, I invite people to journey and go deeper to find their own source of power.

Today, I am working with organizational learning and private teaching where I offer creative programs and workshops that include sculptural processes where we make boats and hearts. One of my favorite workshops to lead is Drawing Meditation that gives one a way to relax and find flow. My program in Close Observation is based on conversations where we look at art together to make new meaning and associations that can add vitality and open visual intelligence in one's life.

My goal is to serve as a facilitator in a number of ways for people to come more alive as they engage with art. I believe that art holds a key for us to deepen our humanity and what we do while on this planet. Art is our earliest way of finding meaning. I cannot imagine any other way I would have had such a richly rewarding life without the help of my muse. She is there 24/7 and is never judgmental. And this muse is available for anyone who has a willing ear to listen.

Sword Fern, Alison Trujillo

Beacon Of Light

Barbara Greensweig

Pictures in the Sky

Kathleen Meadows

As a young child living on a 3-acre farm in the lower San Joaquin Valley, I would spend long days lying in alfalfa fields, the pungent aroma filling my senses as I gazed up at the sky. At dawn it would be pink and gold, sometimes cyan-blue at midday, deepening to violet at nightfall. I would pretend I was an astronomer studying the skies, trying to imagine stories as I scanned my celestial hideaway. I remember wanting to describe my feelings so everyone would know what it was like to watch stars move, or clouds morph into pet sheep—not yet sheared, or the sensation of mud squishing between my toes as I hopped back to our small clapboard house with the wraparound porch.

My imagination became more intense as I grew older. I could scarcely wait for the dented yellow school bus to drop me off so I could race home to make a secret fort out of eucalyptus branches, or watch the Angus bull mating one of our favorite Guernsey cows (a forbidden activity). Holidays were extraordinary events; for me they became visions.

I would see Santa's silhouette, hear his reindeer hooves tracking across the rooftop on Christmas Eve—ignoring my older sister's scoffing that it was only our dad dressed up, carrying a gunnysack. Little did I realize that my father, at thirty-eight, was slowly dying of intestinal cancer. I was too young, not allowed to know. I could still run out to the barn with him before dawn, bring in the frothy milk, warm as it sloshed over the galvanized bucket onto my bare feet, wait patiently as he handed me bottles to feed our newborn lambs, their sucking mouths so powerful I'd have to hold on tight with both hands. Those years everything was exciting and visceral. The truth was kept from me even as my father gradually grew thin and pale, visits to the doctors ever more frequent.

We left our beloved homestead after my mother miscarried, moved into a tract house in the suburbs. My father began teaching agriculture at the local college, wearing colostomy bags strapped under his work pants. Our backyard oil drum became an incinerator for syringes and dressings. After eleven operations and two resuscitations, he remained optimistic, though now entirely bedridden. At thirteen I was vigilant, sitting at his side sharing books, sporting news, stories of our life left behind on the farm —until the nurse would appear with the morphine-filled hypodermic needle. He died that April; he was forty-five. I found myself staring into an abyss of loneliness, filled only by written words. I read until I couldn't see, stumbled through class clutching my memories and my stories.

Teen life was spent in escape—hours bent over the piano (not doing any justice to *Rustle of Spring* or the syncopated jazz of Beiderbecke), discovering Buddhism and Taoism, wandering in silent search for meaning. On my mother's urging to clean my room, I found a faded red diary I had started at my father's bedside. I opened the speckled lock to read, to continue my pain in words. But no ideas came, no stories formed. On wet pages I saw something unexpected—images! I saw the morning light over our barn right before dawn, the way the tall sunflowers drooped backwards on hot days; the flood of sensations—the feel of briars when I fell off my horse, the prick of sharp cotton bolls on my fingers, the smell and taste of alfalfa. I recall feeling so free. I wanted that moment to last forever.

When I entered grad school at UC Berkeley, I had decided to become an English teacher, inspired to work in inner city schools. I started writing about my summer experiences in a housing project—how the kids had never been to a municipal pool, slept in a tent, or eaten s'mores over a campfire. In return, they shared *their* stories with me— how the sound of gunshots at night would keep them awake, where drugs "went down," or how funerals could be as frequent as birthday celebrations. I gave these stories to my supervisor who encouraged me to continue to reach out to these kids, to inspire hope and help create meaningful goals.

Years later, after becoming a teacher in San Francisco, I noticed a sad girl in the middle of my class. She had lost her mother, and I could see the same lost look I had felt years ago. I encouraged her to write, to first visualize her thoughts then put them down on paper, without regard for punctuation. She did, later becoming a known author who gratefully mentioned me in her book. I felt this was reason enough to have chosen this profession. But, rewarding as teaching was, it was also a highly stressful job—accompanied by a grueling commute. As the years progressed, I suddenly found myself an overworked and exhausted mother of three, juggling school and home, alone.

In my twenties I married my dream—stability, the urge to please my family, to fit in. It was my ideal to marry a young, handsome lawyer, an ideal whose shiny veneer hid an ocean of expectation and disappointment. On my own with a small child, I again longed for family cohesion. My neighbor, an avid outdoorsman from a rural farming family, accepted this challenge. Several hiking adventures later, I remarried and birthed two more children. Paradise was short-lived as my life transformed into a marathon of obligation: commuting, shopping, laundry, cooking. Bedtime stories became sacred rituals, time I cherished with my kids. There seemed to be no room, or time, for *me*. That child who saw stories in the sky had vanished. But, as I discovered years later, she was not gone, only dormant.

Two divorces and countless miles of reflection later, I held onto the shining resilience of hope. After four decades in the classroom, I finally retired and ventured into a brand new life of challenges: writing classes at night, poetry salons, belly dancing rehearsals, Chopin on my old Yamaha, and even Chinese brush painting. But it was the music of words, the raw poetry of sight and sound—seeds germinated on a valley farm long ago—that wouldn't let go.

Looking back, it's not been an easy journey—a single mother raising a son and two daughters (all educators). But the hard part has been to become reacquainted with my inner spirit; it has taken some time, along with some pain. I have found strength through my struggle, reawakening my desire to revisit those clouds and stars of my childhood.

Now each time I pick up a journal, I see a new opportunity to create that sense of wonder first evoked by those pictures in the sky.

Backyard Garden

Barbara Greensweig

Essential Goods

Jennifer Fowler Vaida

Over the past months, as we've become all too attuned to the nuances of orange, red, and purple tiering, and we've been living with various degrees of "partial reopening" in fits and starts, it's easy for the early days of the COVID-19 pandemic to fade into a hazy memory.

We might forget the eerie silence of deserted streets—no cars, no pedestrians. (Recall that in those early days, we didn't even venture forth to walk in our own neighborhoods yet; we were sewn up in our houses, waiting "a few weeks" for the all clear.)

We might forget the stark reality of naked supermarket shelves, and checking twitter and text feeds for tips on stores that still had stocks of bread or pasta, fresh produce and bottled water, speeding off to far-flung neighborhoods to score a bag of beans and a crate of canned pineapple chunks. (We never needed bags of beans or crates of canned pineapple before, but these were strange times, strange times indeed. Who knew what we might need to survive? At least we were staving off scurvy.)

Now, if we do remember, we do so with a little chuckle, ha ha, weren't we so silly: standing in line outside Target at 6:30 a.m. because the website announced that a new shipment of toilet paper had arrived the night before—and counting the people ahead of us, calculating our odds of actually getting a pack, scanning to see who might be slow or infirm that we could elbow past to get to the paper goods section before them, giving stink eye to the families that came in a cluster, each of whom could walk away with their own precious package of t.p., reducing the stock available to the rest of us.

(Did I send my Zoom students off to "asynchronous assignments" on a Tuesday afternoon so that I could drive twenty-five miles across the Bay in pursuit of a 36-roll of Charmin Ultra Soft? Oh yes. Yes I did.)

These early days were not a proud moment for humanity. We were truly living in a bunker mentality. Before we were baking sourdough loaves to gift to neighbors or handcrafting our own mandolins to serenade the street, before we started daily walks in our own neighborhoods and actually learned who lived in that corner house with the garden we've always admired—before we realized this state of siege wasn't coming to an end soon and that we would have to make the best of it—before that, our little world was a brutal place to be.

Nothing was open. Nothing. Just grocery stores and Target—and with reduced hours. (Eventually we would get some limited retail and, thank god, take-out, but that didn't happen for several weeks.) Worse, Amazon was prioritizing the shipment of "essential goods." (The price gouging on Amazon was real. And even their supplies were limited. Was I tempted to pay $96 for a 6-pack of Cottonelle with Prime shipping? Only for a moment. Well, a long moment.)

Books were not considered "essential goods."

I'll say that again: books were not considered "essential goods."

No books! With libraries closed, bookstores shuttered, and now Amazon prioritizing butt wipes over literature, it really felt like the End Times.

Our last vestige of humanity, of transcendence, of even just escape—denied.

Now we really were living like animals.

And just when life looked ever so bleak, a dear friend called with an idea. An idea that just might reinfuse our world with humanity. With thoughtfulness. With hope.

My friend set up a "drive-by" library system so her friends could exchange something even more essential than toilet paper: books.

And conversation.

And connection.

I was so, so fortunate to be part of this intimate COVID-lending library. Every couple of weeks, I would pack up a little bag of paperbacks that I had enjoyed and drive up the interstate. There, the garage door would be open and two chairs set up (well-distanced—my friend's son checked out the window from time to time to make sure we didn't inch too close to one another, calling us out if we needed to scootch further away).

I dropped off my bag and picked up the parcel she had left in the garage for me. A bag of lovingly curated books she had enjoyed and that she was now sharing with me. Of course, because of my friend's thoughtfulness, the bag didn't just contain books. There was always a little "something special" that she added: a lovely soap, a chocolate, a lip balm.

And then we would sit—in the weak sun trying to shine through the fog layer—and the real gift unfolded. She and I would talk—normal "girl talk," two friends catching up. Health, husbands, jobs, mutual friends, extended family, and, yes, covid and political news of the day—it all felt so human, so honest.

So real in an unreal world.

Today, we are vaccinated and double-masked and—dare I say it?—facing the possibility of a "green tier" soon. (Did we even know there was a green tier?) And we look back at our sheltered months, recognizing that in a crazy year of politics and pandemic, we had blessings. The blessing of family. The blessing of home. The blessing of time.

And what I will always remember of this past year is the blessing of a folding chair propped open on a lawn and the warm conversation with my dear, dear friend.

My friend who knows that the best way to reach one's humanity is to supply them with books.

And with love.

Changing Woman Navajo Myth

Gretchen Butler

Art Round-Up

Gretchen Butler

During my toddlers' nap time, I glanced around the kitchen and sketched the eggbeater on a whim. My version was askew, which reflected my life. However, the feel of the pencil on paper was pleasing, and the eggbeater metaphor made me smile even though I was in heartbreak mode.

That first drawing fifty years ago opened a path for the can opener, watering can, stove, and ironing board. Then, children, fishermen, petunias, and chickens danced onto pages. Drawings translated into prints from linoleum blocks warmed in the oven, then clamped onto the kitchen table to be carved. The following decades, small increments of art in the kitchen amidst family hubbub saved my sanity.

I especially did not want to take a class. Did not want anyone telling me what to do. Pleasure emerged from allowing shapes to emerge without judgment, without an end product agenda. Well, since I don't like to waste stuff, the first rough prints became stationery for letters to my parents.

I thank my parents for encouraging us to explore our passions—although artwork was not one of them when I was a kid. They had a positive parenting attitude. For example, our family's Three Mistakes Rule applied to rude or clumsy table manners, spilled milk, etc. We had three chances before anyone could nag, criticize, or holler at us. By the time we approached the third "strike," exaggerated drama made the scene a joke. My parents' strategies helped us become conscious of what we did instead of thwarting confidence with angry scare tactics. We grew up willing to ease into new experiences.

As an adult, I was hooked on drawing and printing for six years before the second phase of art development kicked in. A harsh inner critic gained power as I compared myself with artists near and far. Even so, I was hooked on the quiet meditation's play between feelings and shapes on the page. The stack of paintings became so high I had to turn it all into wrapping paper or do something to introduce myself to the world. As the self-imposed deadline approached, I had no idea of what to do. I had an upset stomach on the Day.

I took the stack of paintings into the interior decorator store next to Alpha Beta. The decor featured traditional, realistic still life and landscape art—opposite to my wonky, whimsical style. I did not have an appointment but had nothing to lose. The woman at the desk perused all my work, then proposed a deal. She gave me junk frames, which I sanded and painted to complement my favorite paintings. These pieces received her professional mat/glass fittings so that they were presentable for shows. In exchange, I painted florals with color palettes customized for specific decorators. Hundreds of florals with just barely enough of a unique flair managed to satisfy all of us.

My first show, *Rising Bread Dough*, included a large, red print based on the original eggbeater sketch. After the display in the window of Some Crust Bakery in Claremont, CA, other venues and connections opened up. The arrangement with the interior decorator framer, Leslie Pearson, made possible my participation in dozens of folk venues and professional galleries. Solo shows benefitted the local nature conservancy. Paintings tumbled out in starts and snatches betwixt family and work—my studio was still in the kitchen.

In the third phase of growth as an artist, the witchy self-critic became friends with my inner time-keeper. My three-ring circus juggler took strolls outside the ring. At home, most sessions with the paint were short, but I gave however many sessions necessary for more complex work. The slowdown helped hone technique and ramped up enjoyment. This enhanced a sense of well-being, of living in a larger emotional and spiritual space.

I learned to lighten up—if the work was lousy, paint over it. Sometimes again and again. Equally important, though, was learning to look with soft eyes. What I first thought were mistakes were sometimes gifts. Surprises from paint slurps, slops, spatters, and inaccuracies of all sorts became springboards for a new direction or nuance. Awareness of my own visceral reactions to colors, shapes, and details also provided guidance.

Meditating on the blank page continues to surprise me and help balance my stance with life's perplexing issues. Now that my kids are grown and I've retired from teaching special education, I write, garden, and do art galore. Attention to color, design and texture touches everything: paintings, fabric-wrapped sculptural dolls, garden art, food art, door frames, bathtubs, dustpans, ceilings.

Although my work has sold readily in art centers, boutiques, and bookstores, I will never be professional in the sense that my art is market-driven. Curiosity and exploration lead to shifting subject matter and styles. My stream of work has more than one current, which is a process that runs counter to predictable branding. While each project has earned enough to finance the next, I'm not good at reaching farther than local audiences.

Since the coronavirus has broken the circle of making and sharing art in person, we hope to lasso new ways for connecting private creativity with the larger world. I have four publications, tablets, and sets of colorful stationery boxed up—all of them are too lively to molder away in storage. I'm seventy-seven years old. Maybe I need another self-imposed deadline to start figuring it out.

Path, Jennifer Ewing

My Own Diary

Nitza Agam

My first journal was a Girl Scout Diary my mother bought me at the age of nine. I loved that diary. It had a lock on it which promised me privacy and autonomy. I realized even at that age how my thoughts could truly be my own and had a life outside of me on those pages. In thick, childish cursive which I was still learning, I wrote about what happened to me every day. I still have that diary. It has the picture of a Girl Scout in uniform with long blonde hair and an open diary in front of her, and a pen in her mouth as she ponders what to write. Underneath her image are the words, "My Own Diary." That says it all. "My Own Diary."

The first entry read: "Today is Friday. My name is Nitza. I am a brownie in Troop 442. My leader is Mrs. Fischer. I love meetings on Wednesday." Each page depicts an event of the day. Every entry marks the day of the week including my birthday which is the same day as Passover. It ends with the sentence, "I will have Elijah's cup ready."

Somehow, I knew at the age of nine that writing in a journal would be a way of archiving my life and a way to document and observe: to keep my sanity when life would veer out of control or feel triumphant. It would be a way to mark milestones. The next milestone was a thick, green journal with newspaper articles glued tightly onto the pages about JFK's assassination. It recorded not only the shock and horror but my own way of being part of that history in Newark, New Jersey. I witnessed the assassination of Lee Harvey Oswald on television, and remembered school being closed for a week, glued to the news. Faded newspaper articles glued carefully to pages and pages from that time period reflected the importance of living through history and marking it.

A theme that runs through all my journals is trying to comprehend death. Even at an early age, I experienced the randomness of it while walking through the neighborhood with my mother and witnessing a telephone worker who had been electrocuted above us on the pole. It had happened right in front of us as the man on the pole slumped over. That moment as I looked up and realized this man was dead while holding on to my mother's hand was the first time. I would be trying to confront death over and over again on so many pages of so many journals throughout my life.

When our family moved to Germany when I was eleven, I recorded finding silverware with swastikas on it, and seeing images of concentration camps on German television. Ironically, it was in Germany I first recognized myself as Jewish. My diary became a series of questions and indignation as I confronted my new German friend, Vera, about being Jewish and what happened in Germany during the Holocaust.

"Did you know, Vera, that they killed a lot of Jews here? Did you hear about Hitler and what he did?" I wanted Vera to take responsibility, but she could not. She had no idea what I was talking about. I often think of Vera and myself with our backpacks in fairy tale Germany walking to school interrogating her. At ten years old, I learned to be a conscience.

In high school the diary writing helped me pursue journalism, and I became the editor of the national newspaper of a Zionist youth movement. I learned how to write opinions and to foster a team spirit of writers and to keep deadlines. That editorial was always due every month. I clutched my editorials before the age of e-mails in my purse and took the bus to Manhattan to publish and edit. Writing created an autonomy I could not replicate anywhere else.

Immigrating to Israel and living there for seven years would become the most literary rich period in my writing life, and many journals would cover those years of falling in love with Jerusalem, with the country, and with a young blue-eyed Israeli who shared my name. I rode his motorcycle clutching him from the back, cementing my bond to this country which I adopted and had planned on living in from the moment I saw photos of the concentration camps on German television.

I stood at my boyfriend's father's grave and realized he had died so young and worried that my boyfriend would suffer the same fate. His father had died in a motorcycle accident. I was right to worry. My boyfriend was killed in the Yom Kippur War in 1973 during the first week of the war. He was buried next to his father. Writing became my therapy, my way of healing as I wrote and mourned and cried. It transferred into writing a woman's theatre piece with poetry from my journals about losing a first love at the age of twenty-two. Poetry and theatre and my journals became my refuge.

Moving to San Francisco captured more journals, a different time of exploration as San Francisco served as the antithesis of Israel; a city that cared about love and knew nothing of war, a city of hills and views, and pale greens and blues, wonderful neighborhoods to explore as I found work and studied literature at San Francisco State University. I could lay the grief aside and write about it, but from a distant place and to cry less, to mourn, but not to grieve.

Marriage and motherhood and a new career as a teacher opened up new paths, a new stability as San Francisco became my home and we rented a house, then bought one that we still live in today. More journals and the topic of motherhood, becoming a mother to two sons, and losing my best friend, my mother, after she and my father moved to San Francisco to live closer to my family and me. Grief again became a theme as it opened up wounds of the past and writing poems about my mother became a way to heal, to recover. My grandmother had died two years before my mother, and that female generation of women, strong, complex women who moved continents to create family and to live near their daughters were gone. I was the sole daughter left.

My mother had traveled as much as she could to visit my grandmother after leaving Israel, and then moved to Israel and once she left, ill herself, to be closer to her daughter, she would suffer the guilt of an only daughter who had left her mother. I was guilty that I had not been the daughter I wanted to be because motherhood consumed me. She was there for me, but was I there for her?

I look back at "My Own Diary," that does not seem over fifty years old. The lock might still work if I tried hard enough. The pages stretch over months. Once the months end, I had planned to write more writing, "Dear Diary . . ." on empty pages in preparation for the next month's writing. For some reason, those pages remained empty. The nine-year-old did not return to those pages. But the sixty-nine-year-old cherishes that first attempt at writing which has never stopped.

Woman Rising, Women Honoring Sii (Water)

Catherine Herrera

How the Spirit of Creativity Moves Me

Catherine Herrera

When I was a young artist, still unfamiliar with this energy called Creativity, after each new creation, I wondered, will Creativity show up again? Is it something I can or will up on my own? What brings it forth, what pushes it away? Dipping into the obscurity of the darkroom as a sweat lodge, where I communicated with Creativity, I offered my dedication to the perfect tone and the full Ansel Adams Zone.

Photography was the first of those images pinned to the corkboard in my grandparent's kitchen, with stories of loved ones and where they were now. My Grandpa's travel photos and my dad's first published photos were the first bread crumbs on my path. Before there was a camera, I used my fingers to frame those images I would have taken.

Creativity returned. Again. And, again. I learned to collaborate with the energy, to offer proper deference and respect. I was no idiot. I knew I had no control over Creativity. Patiently, Creativity showed me how we could work together to create magic.

Successfully transmitting the Creative energy from artist to another human being is the first sign one might be able to truly honor Creativity. Becoming the vessel of creative exchange is just the first step, still higher up, connecting universal feeling and experience and impacting positively another life, recognizing the energy flows back to the artist, for I know few greater joys than witnessing Creative energy successfully gifted and received. Promise made, Promise kept.

That is the artist I dream to be.

The first time I was contacted about a portrait I took as a newspaper photographer, I received the money offered for doing the job I considered the best in the world. Invitations to exhibit, invitations to participate. A professional artist—this is all I ever wanted to be. Inspired by women artists I saw making art. If I worked hard, I hoped the same would be for me.

Little did I know, it was not the working hard that would be so difficult.

Chips fell off Creativity, hammered out on myself, internalized statements said outside and apart from my creative being. Definitions of women. Definitions of race. Definitions of class. *"People like us don't become artists."*

I bought my first video camera in secret.

"Wasteful. Who do you think you are?"

I hid those reproaches inside—were they right? Who did I think I was?

I continued. I expanded skills, I opened up new creative mediums, I walked a step forward, despite steps back, celebrated each *paso* as evidence of progress, even when my bank account said zero.

I applied, I applied, I applied, I applied, I applied. I was rejected. I was strong. Apply again. Again rejected. Rejected again.

"See. Told you so. Bum."

Grants. Commissions. Exhibits. Happiest moments in my life—save those personal moments for which, without, none of it matters.

"Congratulations! I always knew you could."

Then, everything changed. A blood draw. A ruined nerve in my right arm traveled to my spine, affecting my legs.

I was a mom. Our lives changed.

Creativity came to the door. "Let's go."

"Are you crazy?" I asked.

"No. Let's go."

Creativity carried me on its shoulders, told me there was a reason to make it through the worst moments and experiences; in fact, Creativity told me to document, draw, write, photograph. Move it!

Soon, and before I knew it, Creativity and I were walking forward once again. Yes. I had to change. Yes. I had to dig deeper. Yes. I had to see with fresh vision.

A new friend asked if I'd photograph her book cover—Nitza Agam—her husband Ofer Agam—shared with me the wisdom he gained—together, encouraging me to hold on tightly to everything I could still do after a life-altering disability. No longer out in the streets documenting, I began working in a studio. Working with authors, even trying photojournalism again. No. Not like before, but Creativity was enough, and I did my best.

I grew to appreciate Creativity in a new way. Creativity—and the love, empathy, kindness of family and friends—kept me alive through some of the most challenging times of my and our lives.

Not just the creativity as creative on commission, but in the ways, Creativity made it possible to process some of the most difficult personal reckonings.

I was obsessed with knowing my family genealogy. A reaction to trauma, reduced to paper, like pushing a wheel endlessly around in circles. I spent a lifetime seeking out who I was so I could know where I am going. There is a saying common to many native and indigenous peoples—*"you cannot know where you are going unless you know where you are from."*

I needed answers to our native/indigenous genealogy for the family, but I needed the answers for myself, and my next generations, to stop this cycle, to be the generation of change our ancestors saw.

Creativity walked with me on that journey, picking up the search from my grandfather, a destination he sought but never found. Was I doomed to never know?

"Who are you to tell this story? Where is your proof? What is your percentage?"

Tracing Maria, Indian, from the 1852 census, finding my great-great-great-grandpa born in San Francisco in 1857, and learning how my family intermarried and were family to members of the Rumsen, Esselen, Mutsun Ohlone community, researching the story of our family and stories of being Ohlone became my obsession creatively too.

Then, others told me they had similar experiences, and Creativity put up a mirror. I began making movies about my family and my journey, broadening out to make movies and art no longer just about me or my family; with permission and the participation of Ohlone community members, sacred sites, and the mission practice of using wooden dolls as punishment.

Creativity made it possible to heal, to grieve for all that I lost, pushing me to learn all that I had not been taught.

I did not withdraw the search for my relatives. New documents, new DNA. These were not just rumors and myths but the result of colonization, opening my eyes to the ways today the same wheel is spinning round and round.

Creativity and I look forward to the next chapter, picking up projects put on hold, a documentary about Martins Beach, finishing a book about my journey tracing both sides of my family's native genealogy and stories, and developing a T.V. series. Creativity and I ask, how can we add to the healing, more so now in these days and times.

Trauma is funny that way, making it hard to move at the times when most needed.

Creativity roused me awake, grabbed me by the hand, "Time to move forward," and off we go, down a new path, up a different street, around the same circle, for a lifetime—as long as Creativity returns for another dance.

.

Grotte, Jennifer Ewing

To the Moon
for Bernadette Track

Abby Caplin

Where O'Keefe painted
a burnished clay barrette,
the sky blooms in celestial
turquoise—a ghost ladder
plucked from Taos, plunged
into charged landscape. Half-pearl,
half-lidded moon of mica beckons,
invisible ancestors dancing upward
over lacquered hills
to another world,
               while still-breathers
kneel near Rio Pueblo, build
pit fires, fashion horsehair
onto hot clay, some recalling
the time they fed Easy Rider's
film crew, flirted with Fonda
as motorcycles smoked through Taos.
In summer heat, an elder
ferries memories of R. C. Gorman
from her closet—
the gallery of velvets, crimson
and purple, the wardrobe
she modeled for his paintings.
A master potter, she balances
a heart of earth in her palm
until it pulses with Red Willow

song, sponging the newborn pot
in a slip of grandmothers—
adobe home of a thousand
years, storied ladders of spruce . . .

Bernadette Track is a potter, painter, actress, and an elder of the Taos Pueblo. A graduate of the Institute of American Indian Art, she studied dramatic arts at Julliard and was a founding member of the Native American Theater Ensemble, performing in off-Broadway productions. She was a founder of the Taos Pueblo Children's Theater, a model for Navajo artist R.C. Gorman, and has taught micaceous clay classes at the University of New Mexico-Taos. A master potter, her works can be found in the Albuquerque Museum, galleries, and private collections.

A different version of this poem was first published in In Good Works Review, 2020.

Moon Over Taos

Alison Trujillo

Following D.H. Lawrence

Nitza Agam

I got on a small, wooden chair outside this simple cottage near Taos, New Mexico, and tried to look inside to learn more about D.H. Lawrence's life. The cottage was closed to visitors, but I was determined to get a glimpse of the interior. I hoped I wouldn't be accused of loitering or trespassing. On the wall of the cottage were paintings done by Lawrence, and I was able to see some of them: his erotic portraits of men and women signed "Lorenzo." It was one of those moments you record in your head: the moment I stood on a bench in the oppressive heat of New Mexico looking into a window where this famous author had painted and lived. I could almost imagine him and Frieda talking, working, as I breathed in their past life.

I had reached the Lawrence Ranch that morning as my roommate and I drove up the winding road which led to the ranch. I smelled eucalyptus and pine and thought of Jerusalem where I had lived for seven years and of the Israeli desert. My past was catching up to me in this brilliant New Mexico light. The ranch was rustic and did not look very different than it did in 1924 when D.H. Lawrence and his wife, Frieda, settled there. The cabin they lived in was a simple building, and the path behind it led to a series of steps to the white shrine with a phoenix, a symbol of renewal in Lawrence's work, sitting up on the front roof. The large initials DHL were carved into the concrete of the block.

Once inside the shrine is a sign in guest register to the left. People had signed their names and written personally to D.H. Lawrence. I wrote: "I am with you, D.H., asking, experiencing, wondering, questing, dreaming, and loving." I could see what drew Lawrence to this place. New Mexico with its golden light, scents of pine trees, starry, clear nights and a bright white moon, reflected his love for life even as he wrote about characters in gray, gloomy England. I loved Lawrence for the way he wrote about women: they were strong, sexual characters who were not afraid to fulfill their innermost desires.

The first time I saw some of D.H. Lawrence's paintings was in Taos at the La Fonda De Taos Inn where my friend and I were staying, when the owner, Saki, invited me to his room. Saki was a famous character of Taos, nicknamed the "Don Juan of Taos," and he had mixed with the famous, the rich and the literary: the old time Taos artists, movie stars, foreign diplomats, and local and international friends who had all congregated at this hotel painted in shades of blue. My room at La Fonda was painted blue; the walls of the lobby were blue in stark contrast to the intense gold and brown of the desert surrounding Taos.

Saki, true to his nickname, made a habit of inviting young women to his room. I was no exception, and I sat in his cluttered room full of portraits, paintings, shelves of books, and knickknacks. He showed me dusty D.H. Lawrence novels signed by Frieda and dedicated to Saki; he told me that he and Picasso had shared a certain Swedish lover. Saki invited my roommate and me to swim with him that night at one of his friend's homes. We agreed to meet and drive with him to the home outside Taos.

It was a magical evening. Either no one lived at this house or they were gone. We swam in the pool on a dark, starry night illuminated by the moon and millions of stars. The stars were clear and they filled the night. Saki spoke to us about the old days and the home of some long-forgotten movie star as we swam. New Mexico, to me, that night, was about nature and sky and colors and art and artists and writers and spirits of the past. It was about my own erotic longing and fantasies, of becoming a writer while at the same time being a mother and a teacher. Here in the desert, at the Lawrence Ranch, or even in the blue-roomed inn, I could allow myself to be the lover, the Native American, the Jew, the Catholic, the wanderer, and the writer, the women in D.H. Lawrence's novels.

I knew I was at a juncture, mother of two sons approaching adolescence, a husband whose diagnosed MS would probably worsen, and a mother who was slowly dying of her illness which had plagued her from her early forties. I was teaching at a private school, and while I loved children and teaching, I was not becoming the writer I thought I might be.

I would end my journey to New Mexico with a trip to the simple church of Chimayo, which was known for its "holy dirt" providing healing for the ill. My mother suffered in San Francisco from a terrible, mutilating disease. She had been a woman of bright, flamboyant colors and jewelry and bright red and orange lipsticks. She loved to dress up, while I, in contrast, usually wore muted browns and grays. Now I was alive once more in the sultry heat of New Mexico, inspired to write, and to bring her holy dirt, in the hope that she would return to her former self. I wanted my young, beautiful mother back. Perhaps the dirt would resurrect her as my spirit was resurrected in the heat, the desert, the Lawrence Ranch, and Taos.

I watched a woman scoop up the dirt gingerly and pour it into a special bag as if it were gold. People came from all over the state and the country to collect this healing dirt; they rubbed themselves with it, they prayed over it, they brought it to those who needed healing. I hoped this holy dirt would help my mother. I asked the woman who noticed me observing her.

"Will this help my mother?"

"If you believe, it will help," she answered.

I brought the dirt to my mother in San Francisco. She smiled when I gave it to her and I told her the story of Chimayo Chapel. I wanted her to receive some of that sacred space of New Mexico, the red chili peppers that appeared everywhere, the pinks and golds of the desert, the stark, simple crosses on the chapels and churches, the bright blue of the hotel room and the cloudless sky, the white moon in a dark, starry night. My mother died a year later. Did it help heal her?

I know my pilgrimage helped me heal as I remembered the eccentricity of Saki, Lawrence's cabin and his erotic paintings, the blue, blue rooms of La Fonda de Taos, the town of Taos. I prayed at Chimayo Chapel for my mother, for my husband, for my two children, for myself to continue to take in D.H. Lawrence's spirit who was similarly changed by the light and feel of New Mexico. I felt confident that I would eventually write and become that writer that I knew I could be.

Aqua Corraline

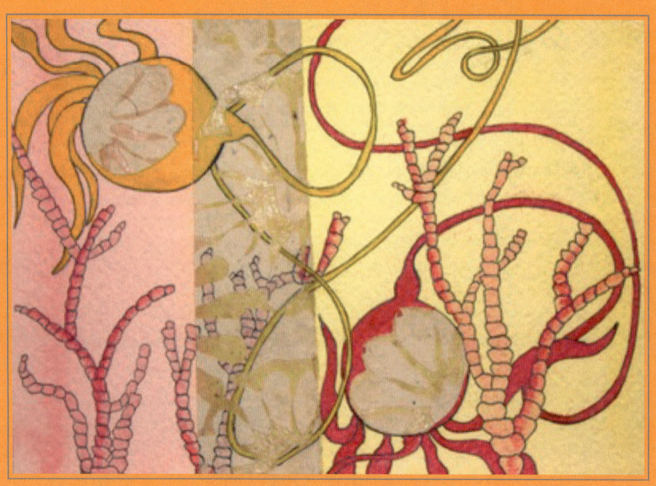

Alison Trujillo

To the Creatives

Alison Trujillo

To my maternal grandmother, whose home had an entire wall of colorful yarn skeins and rooms adorned with her weavings. To my paternal grandfather who wrote me letters with collage pieces mixed in among the words and who sanded and stained pieces of driftwood until they shone to perfection at his woodworking bench. To my maternal grandfather who, despite his own claims of clumsiness, managed to create vivid, mini Chinese-opera stage sets upon which we made tiny puppets dance and sing.

To my mother whose quilts teach me about that perfect balance between precision and flow, whose Amish-style blankets always leave one imperfect piece, like life itself. To my father, who sings and strums the guitar and who coaxes native plants to flourish among roses and a plum tree; to my friend Marcia, whose whimsical garden additions—a curled trellis here, a wooden duck head there—make wandering among the vegetable beds a delight. To my father-in-law who rises before the sun to brew a pot of coffee, spending his mornings among pine, madrone, and cedar in the woodshop.

Thank you.

To the art studio I enjoyed during my twenties: a space to create and cavort with fellow creative souls, each of us so different in process and outcome, each of our red tool carts filled to the brim with paper, paints, medium, brushes. Tired from a long day of work, I would somehow gain new energy when walking through that building's heavy doors. For the young woman from Santa Fe who sold me her plastic shelving unit filled with acrylics, in the hopes that this fellow artist could put them to use.

For the privilege to see art in the Louvre, the Uffizi, the Alhambra, the manicured gardens of French chateaus and the rambling roses over English gates. For the community murals that fill my soul when I walk by. For the painting teacher who swooned over everyone else's perfect, life-like portraits but mine, leading me to find a different style for my voice.

Thank you.

To my husband who embraces the idea of my little art studio in the redwoods, which I enjoy today—smiling to myself when I disappear down the path and through the red studio door for a couple of hours. Getting there can be more difficult than a simple walk down the rickety steps. Work, house projects, and my beautiful, loveable, energetic dog are all vying for my attention. And then there is the self-doubt, which itself could be an entire essay. But then there is the moment when I look up through the trees to the moon . . . or at the colorful grasshopper resting on the grass . . . or the swirling kelp in the sea . . . and I know I have to draw them, paint them, and somehow document their beauty to make them my own. This means I can thank myself—for listening amid the din of life.

And to my fellow artists, always: writers, painters, photographers, ceramicists . . . sharing ideas in this churning current, so that we each may scoop up some of that water and drink—to quench the days of frustration and nights of little inspiration, taking each other's gifts and making them our own, proving that these voices, our voice, yearns to be heard.

Thank you.

Pumpkin Pickup

Barbara Greensweig

Green River

Jennifer Ewing

A Beautiful Life

Angela Neff

There are movies that change lives. *Life is Beautiful*, a 1997 Italian film directed by Roberto Benigni, changed mine.

The film is about a father, determined to save his young son, Joshua, from the brutal reality of the concentration camps. He does so by convincing his son that their life is actually a game where the winner will get his very own army tank. The film is also about Joshua's non-Jewish mother, Dora, who will not just stand by and watch her family be taken away. When it is clear that there is nothing she can do to save them, she boards the train with them and ends up in the women's quarters of their camp.

My daughter was five years old when this film was released. It revealed to me that by choosing to raise her Jewish, I was also putting her in societal danger in a way that I, a very lapsed Catholic, had not experienced. (Though sadly there is some history, as many Catholics were murdered in the Holocaust.) How could I be willing to risk her safety and not my own? I knew that if I were in Dora's situation, I would have gotten on that train. So I committed to becoming the best kind of upstander I could for my daughter: I became a Jew.

But I didn't do it right away, partly because I was not really sure how. Converts to Christianity just have to say they want to be saved, and "boom," they are. In the Jewish tradition, converts are evaluated for sincerity and have to demonstrate that they will persist in the face of rejection. It is a serious endeavor. Once you are a Jew—you are a Jew for life. This was a much more profound commitment than my previous religious switch from Catholicism to a Methodist liberation theology.

But Judaism is a whole other ball game. It is not just a religion—it is a culture. A culture into which I was not certain I or my daughter would ever be completely accepted. Community is a very important part of any religion. We long to be a part of something larger than ourselves. Though the people who worked at the temple were incredibly welcoming, the broader community felt out of reach. For many people, my (fake) blonde hair, (real) blue eyes, and name make it impossible for them to see me as Jewish—no matter how many times I tell them I am.

When my daughter started her studies at our temple, I studied alongside her and fell passionately in love with Judaism. My commitment to becoming a Jew completely crystallized. Now, I would be choosing it first and foremost out of a deep respect and reverence. A few years later, she and I were interviewed by a beit din and sent to the mikveh, where we immersed in the waters and officially became Jews. That was seventeen years ago, but my Jewish journey started long before that. We participated in Passover, Rosh Hashana, Yom Kippur, Hanukka, and sometimes Sukkot, from the day she was born. I believe my daughter was born with a "neshama"—a Jewish soul. But still there are many Jews who deny her this.

Being a Jew is like any committed relationship. We need to recommit regularly. Lean in to the hard stuff and relish the good. To have a framework for a life of reflection is something we treasure and living outside the Roman calendar makes us more aware of time and meaning. Raising a Jewish child has been one of the most rewarding parts of motherhood. She knows who she is in a way most gentiles do not, and so do I. Life is Beautiful.

Summer Sunflowers, Taos, Alison Trujillo

Below the Mountains

Alison Trujillo

The Changing Light

Kathleen Meadows

Last night I saw the changing light
pink-luster like the inside of a conch shell
hauled from the beach, collecting time
its shell crystals primordial dust—
perhaps the last gasp of a dying galaxy,
small pinpricks of ancient light
cascading through my pupils, flowing
like water carving the hillsides
behind Mt. Tam.

I stood and watched the clouds of Marin,
moving methodically over the hills,
like a medieval scholar scouring the heavens.
I could see across the bay, find my rooftop,
touch the tips of my tallest redwood trees, spot
my cat playing with a fallen baby squirrel.

I saw the light change to deep crimson at the
horizon, soft purple bands melting silhouettes
sharpening my gaze on the fog-blanketed Headlands,
lights from the red bridge haloed across Sausalito
motioning me back to the last waning light above,
the first stars stitched onto blue-black tapestry
like primitive beacons, signaling me home.

First published in Wayfinding: A collection of poetry from Parks and Points online series by Finishing Line.

Biographies

Abby Caplin's poems have appeared in *AGNI, Catamaran, Manhattanville Review, Midwest Quarterly, Salt Hill, The Southampton Review*, and elsewhere. She has been a winner of the Soul-Making Keats Literary Competition, a finalist for the Rash Award in Poetry, and a nominee for Best New Poets. She is a physician in San Francisco. *http://abbycaplin.com*

Alison Trujillo lives in rural, coastal Sonoma County, California. She takes most of her inspiration from the natural world. Her hope is that her work will help to bring appreciation for, and inspire protection of, our beautiful earth. She uses a variety of media, such as watercolors, acrylics, collage elements, and encaustic.

Angela Neff is a California educator, writer, and actor struggling to determine how she can best contribute to solving the social and environmental crises the world is facing today. She lives with her cat MeMe overlooking the Santa Susannah mountains at the intersection of the Los Angeles and Ventura county.

Avigile Gottlieb lives in a moshav in southern Israel. She enjoys expressing herself in various art forms such as painting, and sculpting in clay. Her latest collection is "the woman in the red scarf."

Barbara Greensweig is inspired by the beauty of the vineyards and coast of Northern California where she has lived. Her vibrant landscapes in oil capture the joy of moments in time as she paints scenes of nature "en plein air."

Catherine Herrera lives in San Francisco, California, influenced by generations of artists in her family, documenting our times and creating inspiring visions for the future.

Cynthia Chin Lee is a speaker and author who has published eight books including the best-selling *Amelia to Zora: Twenty-six Women Who Changed the World* and *Operation Marriage*. You can see her website at *cynthiachinlee.com*. Cynthia lives in the San Francisco Bay area and likes walking on the beach, biking, and eating delicious vegan foods.

Darshell McAlpine's love of reading good books grew into a love of writing and publishing them. Her book *Leaving with My Marbles: Finding the Courage to Walk Away Intact* was released in 2018. She is also the owner of Boss Lady Press, an independent book publisher in Houston. *www.bossladypress.com*

Dawn Gibson-Winder is a Mindful Living Designer & Self-Care Coach. Dawn is inspired by the beauty of the botanicals she finds on her walks around her home in the U.K. Her work involves inspiring people who are looking to live a simpler, slower, and calmer lifestyle.

Doreen Stock, poet, memoir artist, and literary translator from Fairfax, CA, hopes to bring aging women into the forefront with her poem to her great-granddaughter, recently published in CATAMARAN, Summer 2021, and *Bye Bye Blackbird,* (thePoetryBox, 2020) poems of her mother's last years.

Gretchen Butler's artwork and life with her husband, Jim, are nestled between forest and meadow in Northern California wildlands. See stories, art, and books at *gretchenbutler.com*.

Jennifer Ewing creates art of spirit that ignites connections between us what is at the core of our beings. Her main symbol is the Spirit Boat that brings in an invitation to experience a journey full of soul. She lives in an SF artist's community where she makes art, holds workshops, and designs programs for self growth.

Jen Vaida writes, teaches, coaches, and wonders aloud in the Bay Area.

Kathleen Meadows, poet, memoirist, artist, and belly dancer, lives in the El Cerrito Hills overlooking the San Francisco Bay. A teacher of many years, she has taught in schools throughout the Bay Area. Growing up in the rural San Joaquin Valley, her experiences inform both her writing and her passion for drawing wildlife. Her poem *The Changing Light* recently appeared in the anthology *Wayfinding* (Finishing Line Press, 2021).

Leigh Verrill-Rhys holds an M.A. in Literature & Language Arts (Creative Writing). Her first legacy-published novel was acquired in 2010 by Avalon Books. She has since published ten more novels and is working on a twelfth and several more. She is also the editor of three autobiographical collections written by women, published in Wales. Leigh lives and writes in Montana.

Marisa Handler—writer, singer-songwriter, teacher, and coach—is the author of the memoir *Loyal to the Sky*, which won a Nautilus Gold Award for world-changing books. She's always been a fan of green eggs and ham.

Marlene Shigekawa, a writer, screenwriter, and film producer and director, is the author of children's books *Blue Jay in the Desert* and *Welcome Home Swallows* and is also the producer for the documentary film, *For the Sake of the Children*. She is in pre-production for her short narrative film about her family's experience in the Japanese American incarceration camps.

Susan E. Light, MD: After practicing pediatric hematology/oncology for several years, Susan moved to a career in clinical drug development, working to get innovative new drugs approved. Her writing reflects a blending of her personal and professional lives.

Nitza Agam

Nitza lives outside San Francisco looking out at her lush lemon tree every morning for comfort and inspiration. She is a writer, poet, educator, mother, wife, and friend to many amazing women! She looks to women's writing and art for community and creativity.

Made in the USA
Middletown, DE
15 July 2022

69473942R00064